P9-ELO-143

HOW I WENT FROM 28 TO SCRATCH IN ONE YEAR PLAYING ONCE A WEEK

AT THE AGE OF 70

BY JOHN YOUNGBLOOD

PRICE STERN SLOAN

Los Angeles

© 1990 by John Youngblood

Published by Price Stern Sloan, Inc.
360 N. La Cienega Boulevard, Los Angeles, California 90048
Printed in U.S.A.

9 8 7 6 5 4 3 2 1

All rights reserved. No part of this publication may be reproduced, stored in a retrieval system or transmitted, in any form or by any means, electronic, mechanical, photocopying, recording or otherwise, without the prior written permission of the publisher.

Library of Congress Cataloging-in-Publication Data

Youngblood, John.
    How I went from 28 to scratch in one year playing once a week—
at the age of 70 / by John Youngblood.
      p.   cm.
    ISBN 0-8431-2830-5
    1. Golf.   I. Title.   II. Title: How I went from twenty-eight to
scratch in one year playing once a week— at age seventy.
GV965.Y63   1990
796.352'3—dc20   90-35066
                                           CIP

The author and publisher are not responsible for and make no representations, warranties, recommendations, endorsements or promises of any kind, either express or implied, regarding the safety, testing, effectiveness, durability, function, manufacture or availability of the products and other items appearing in this book. Furthermore, the author and publisher do not guarantee that this technique will have a direct effect on lowering handicaps.

Recognizing the importance of preserving that which has been written, Price Stern Sloan, Inc. has decided to print this book on acid-free paper, and will continue to print the majority of the books it publishes on acid-free paper.

To every person who has touched golf clubs and
to those who plan to touch golf clubs in the future,
this book is dedicated.

About the Author

John Youngblood is a business executive who has played golf for thirty years. In his early years, he played to a 4 handicap. Then a back injury stopped all his golf activity for five years. Starting golf again, Youngblood found he had a mental block against turning and a problem breaking 100. He arranged a series of lessons with Dave Anderson, a PGA teaching pro. He couldn't break the mental block, so the lessons were unsuccessful. Believing that playing and practice could produce results, he played twice a week and finally attained a 10 handicap, but became stalemated there.

Through extensive research on all golf swings, he developed the Ultimate Golf Swing Fundamentals. Deciding to make a final try to rebuild his game, he started with putting, developing a program of learning and practice. This was so successful that he developed a program of learning and practice for every club. He realized that each golf stroke is only slightly longer than the previous stroke. The programs developed with each club became the Stairstep Learning and Practice Program, which provides the backbone of instruction in this book.

After progressing through the game with each club, Youngblood's handicap began to drop, and finally the great day arrived when it became scratch. Discussing this program with the famous professional teacher George Lumsden, he suggested that this system was "foolproof" and that it should be made available in a book. Thus, *How I Went from 28 to Scratch in One Year Playing Once a Week at the Age of 70* was born.

About Paul Azinger

Paul Azinger, age thirty, was the PGA Tour's 1987 "Player of the Year." Azinger won the PGA Tour's highest award by winning three tournaments, placing second in tour earnings, first in sand saves and the second lowest overall scoring average on the 1987 PGA Pro Playing Tour. Azinger's point total for the PGA Tour's Player of the Year award was sixty-six points. Azinger won the Phoenix Open, the Las Vegas Panasonic Invitational and the Sammy Davis, Jr. Greater Hartford Open and placed third in the Hawaii Open and second in the British Open.

Currently the leading player on the PGA Pro Tour, Azinger's success is underlaid with years of hard work in playing his way to the top. He played college golf and qualified for the PGA Tour three times, but lost his playing card due to low earnings. Undaunted, he was back on the tour in 1984 to stay. In 1987, he finished second on the Tour players' money list. Along the way, Azinger's fans nicknamed him "The Zinger." Now a superstar on the PGA Tour, Azinger has served notice that he is a force to be reckoned with in future tournaments.

CONTENTS

Foreword   vi
Preface   vii
Acknowledgments   viii

Introduction   Golf Is My Challenge   1

Chapter 1   Golf: The Game   21

Chapter 2   Golf Clubs and Equipment   31

Chapter 3   The Stairstep Learning and   39
               Practice Program

Chapter 4   The Ultimate Golf Swing Fundamentals   145

Chapter 5   Shots for Playing Golf   173

Chapter 6   Techniques   179

Chapter 7   Golf Concepts and Terminology   193

Foreword

How I Went from 28 to Scratch in One Year Playing Once a Week at the Age of 70 by John Youngblood provides sound instruction to improve your golf ball striking ability and reduce your scores. His Stairstep Learning and Practice Program describes a natural progression of the skills required to get better at golf. This book is easy to read and understand. If followed, this plan will help just about anyone get his or her handicap down and enjoy the game more. In the photos, I have tried to demonstrate the proper execution of the principles he proposes. I hope they help bring the written word to life.

Becoming a better golfer requires plenty of hard work, but if you have the desire, this book will serve as a good guide. Follow it closely and I'm sure that as your scores get lower, golf will be a lot more fun for you. After all, that's what the game of golf is intended to be—fun.

—Paul Azinger
The PGA Tour's 1987 "Player of the Year"

Preface

How I Went from 28 to Scratch in One Year Playing Once a Week at the Age of 70 was written by a duffer for duffers, who are stalemated at scores between 90 and 100 and who want very much to reduce their handicaps. This book is also written for those of all ages who want to learn to play golf.

This book has been thoroughly researched and is written to serve as a textbook for learning golf and its benefits. Set the goal that you desire to accomplish and use the Ultimate Golf Swing Fundamentals and the ultimate learning and practice program, the Stairstep Learning and Practice Program, to accomplish these goals.

The lifelong benefits of the game of golf are worthy of the price.

—John Youngblood

The author (left) and PGA Tour's "Player of the Year," Paul Azinger, at Rolling Hills Golf Resort, Plantation, Florida.

Acknowledgments

To Paul Azinger and his father, Ralph Azinger, for their additions and corrections which improved the quality of this manuscript. To Paul Azinger, for the photos illustrating the book and for his endorsement. I am proud of Azinger's 1987 achievement and my work with him in the production of this book. Azinger's earning of the PGA Tour's "Player of the Year" was for the best record by a tour playing pro in 1987. Congratulations, Paul, on a great job well done!

To Jerry Shelke, Director of Golf at Rolling Hills Golf Resort, Plantation, Florida. Jerry arranged for the photos of Paul Azinger to be taken at Rolling Hills Golf Resort.

To Tom Thurston, Apogee Photographic, Inc., Fort Lauderdale, Florida. Tom took the photographs of Paul Azinger used for the interior and the back of the jacket of *How I Went from 28 to Scratch in One Year Playing Once a Week at the Age of 70.*

To Marlene Moran, Fort Lauderdale, Florida, for superior typing and diligent work in preparing the manuscript.

INTRODUCTION

Golf Is My Challenge

"If I played golf like John, I would give up the game." The words came like a clap of thunder from some tall bushes, where I had pushed my drive on the 3rd hole of Plantation Golf Club in Plantation, Florida. I recognized the voice as that of an elder in our church, and what made it so incredible was the fact that his game, with a 28 handicap, was no better than mine. I was stunned and hurt by those words, for I deeply respected the man who spoke them. I little realized the profound impact that those words would have on my future actions in golf.

I was president of Plantation Golf Club that year, and we were playing our last tournament of the year. The PGA (Parkway Golf Association), as we call our group, are golfers from the Parkway Christian Church, who play in a tournament once a month. Prizes are awarded for the "Longest Drive," "Closest to the Pin," "Low Gross" and "Low Net." The golfers who win the most in monthly tournaments received a yearly trophy at a final banquet at the end of the season. I had won "Closest to the Pin" the preceding year. We finished the last tournament, and that evening we gathered at the Tropical Acres Restaurant in Fort Lauderdale, Florida for our banquet.

After the meal I signaled for silence and the awarding of the yearly trophies began. The "Longest Drive," "Closest to the Pin" and "Low Gross" were awarded. I won "Low Net," and my trophy was awarded by Ray, an elder in the church and a good friend of mine. The elder, who spoke the words on the golf course that day, didn't win a trophy that night. It was some satisfaction to win the Low Net trophy. However, my 28 handicap made the victory somewhat hollow.

That night we also elected new officers. I was nominated for a second term, and in the nominating speech I was told that I was the best president they ever had. I refused, stating that I either had to give more attention to my game or give it up. How true and how near these words were to coming to pass was to undergird my struggle to play decent golf at a 4 handicap again. I had become a senior citizen that year, but luckily I had kept myself in fine physical shape with diet and exercise. I decided to rest over the Christmas holiday and then begin my assault on lowering my handicap.

I decided to seek the services of a PGA pro. Dave Anderson was the pro at Jacaranda Country Club, in Plantation, Florida. We discussed my problems, and I told him that my back injury had recovered through physical therapy, but that I had been left with a mental block against turning my hips. Dave felt that we could overcome this problem and we arranged for ten lessons. I started with great anticipation. Dave checked my grip and stance, and said they were good. We worked on my backswing, downswing, impact and follow-through. Each lesson consisted of a warm up with the 5 iron, then work with the short irons and later the long irons. Toward the last lesson, we worked with the woods and for some reason I relaxed with the woods and each shot was near perfect. Dave said, "You hit beautiful wood shots, now just practice the irons until you can hit them the same way."

The irons gave me trouble; when I changed clubs, it took several tries to start hitting good shots. Dave said that my swing was "basically good" and thought practice was the answer. But I wasn't completely satisfied. I was eager to play good golf again and the iron shots worried me a great deal.

I decided to remedy the situation by playing twice each week. I soon learned that the benefit of regular play was to transfer my attention to playing the course and solving the course problems. I began to aim my shots to areas where the following shots could be easier. Ever so gradually my handicap began to drop. I broke 90, then settled around 83, where I became stalemated. I wondered if I would ever break 80 again.

To play twice each week required that I get up early and be the first to register in order to fill in with a group that had a missing player. I usually made a tee-off with one of the first three groups. I played just as the sun came up, and the first nine holes were wet, so I had to learn to play a wet weather game. I played with all kinds of golfers—young and old—with handicaps from scratch to 28. I didn't gamble, so most of the players left me alone. Many times they were surprised at my good wood shots and mediocre iron shots. It was while I was filling in that I first played with fellow golfer Ty Weller. He shot 83, and invited me to lunch with him after our round.

Ty and I became friends and we decided to play early each Thursday and have lunch together afterward. I marvelled at Ty's courage. He had phlebitis, which is an inflammation of the veins, and had to wrap his legs before playing golf. Ty hit a lot of good shots and I found it nip and tuck to beat him about every other time. We both were stalemated around 83. Ty and I ended our association after he took a long vacation to North Carolina. I told him I had decided not to play on a regular basis during the coming season.

I became despondent about my game. With all the hard playing I had done, I felt my handicap should be lower. I thought about my situation long and hard and I began to say to myself, "Maybe it is time for me to quit the game."

I continued to exercise and decided to develop golf exercises and work them into my regular routine. I posed in all positions with a 5 iron before a full-length mirror. One day, as I swung the club from the stance to the backswing position, I noticed my right knee quivering and moving back and forth. Of course, this accounted for many errant shots. The right leg must stay flexed and firm and not move during the backswing. I developed control of my right knee to remedy this problem. To help my turn, I began to exercise, turning around my spine. I became good at this and eventually began to shift my weight naturally and at the proper time.

I wanted to keep my hand in golf, so I decided to play once a week and practice in the middle of the week. I concentrated on turning and on keeping my left leg still. My scores began to drop; I broke 80, and 79 became my new goal each time I played. Now encouraged, I decided to make a final assault on the game of golf.

During my working years, I had supervised a lot of research with my research staff. I decided to study every prominent golfer who ever played the game and list the things common to most of them. This study was to cover golf from its inception. My vision was clear. Galloping out of all these statistics, would come the Ultimate Golf Swing Fundamentals, distilled from the essence of every golf swing and shot by pro and amateur alike. This is precisely what I did. I constructed spread sheets, researched golfers and selected the fundamentals common to most of the golfers. From this data came the Ultimate Golf Swing Fundamentals.

The Ultimate Golf Swing Fundamentals

The Grip

The Vardon grip is the most commonly used golf grip. The key in this grip is that the little finger of the right hand overlaps the index finger of the left hand.

Address for the Drive

1. Keep the feet shoulder width apart.
2. Turn the target foot left one-quarter.
3. Straighten the rear foot or keep turned right one-eighth.
4. Flex the knees.
5. Keep the elbows close together.
6. Straighten the arms, but not so they are rigid.
7. Straighten the left arm.
8. Keep the right arm soft.
9. Bend forward from the hips until the weight is on the balls of the feet.

Backswing

Move the triangle of the shoulders, arms and hands, coordinated with the hips, straight back from the ball past the right foot and continue upward to a full backswing. The wrists will cock naturally above the head. The shoulders will turn fully and the back will face the target. The hips turn also. The club will point over the right shoulder toward the target. The club may be taken back to horizontal.

Downswing

The downswing begins by turning the left hip to the left, which causes the target heel to lower and the weight to begin to transfer to the target leg. This drops the triangle of the shoulders, arms and hands toward the waist and the rear foot, as the arms and hands move into the hitting area, below the waist. The left hand will be guiding and the right hand will be ready to smash the ball.

Impact

The swing is down and through the ball. The club head contacts the ball slightly on the upswing, sweeping the ball off the tee. The body position at impact is approximately the same as it was at address.

Follow-Through

The swing should be done around a steady spine. The address posture stays the same throughout the swing. As the triangle moves downward through impact the right arm straightens and both arms are extended toward the target. The weight transfers to the target foot and pulls the body around to face the target. The left arm breaks and the club finishes high over the left shoulder.

These are the fundamentals which evolved from my research. I decided to test them by playing once each week and practicing five hours in the middle of each week. After a month on this program my handicap dropped to 4 again and at long last my full confidence was regained.

Encouraged by my success with the Ultimate Golf Swing Fundamentals, I decided to develop an ultimate practice and learning program.

I realized that putting was the foundation of good golf. I thought of a system to dramatize this for the player who desired to improve his or her handicap, and which would also be serviceable for a beginner learning the basic skills of golf.

I thought about the fourteen clubs used to play the game, and one day it came to me. I said, "The putt is the basic stroke and the stroke for a chip is only slightly longer than the putt." The same is true as we go up the ladder of the clubs. Suddenly, the stairstep idea was born. The Stairstep Learning and Practice Program is that ultimate program.

The Stairstep Learning and Practice Program

This program requires practice to perfect every shot possible with each of the clubs listed on each step before moving to the step above.

The Ultimate Golf Swing Fundamentals and the Stairstep Practice and Learning Program are the foundation for all the instructions and information that follow in this book.

The stairstep program means exactly that. The program begins with putting, and the next step up the stairway to chipping should not be taken until every putting stroke and putting problem has been mastered. Such will be the case while climbing up each step of the stairway. Skipping steps will destroy the program.

Each step must be learned to perfection to form the foundation for the next step. Diligence in executing this program will produce just one thing. It will make a golfer out of you!

I attacked the stairstep program with a vengeance. With this program I would perfect every shot possible with each club needed to play scratch golf.

The Jacaranda Country Club has a beautiful layout of two courses, the west course and the east course. This club also has the finest practice facilities in that part of Florida. There is a 36-hole practice green on the back side, where putting, chipping and short pitch shots can be practiced. The driving range is all grass, with a sand trap and practice green nearby. In these beautiful surroundings, I began to practice for five-and-one-half hours every Wednesday and playing golf once each week.

The following is a precise account of my work with each step on the stairway.

THE STAIRSTEP LEARNING AND PRACTICE PROGRAM

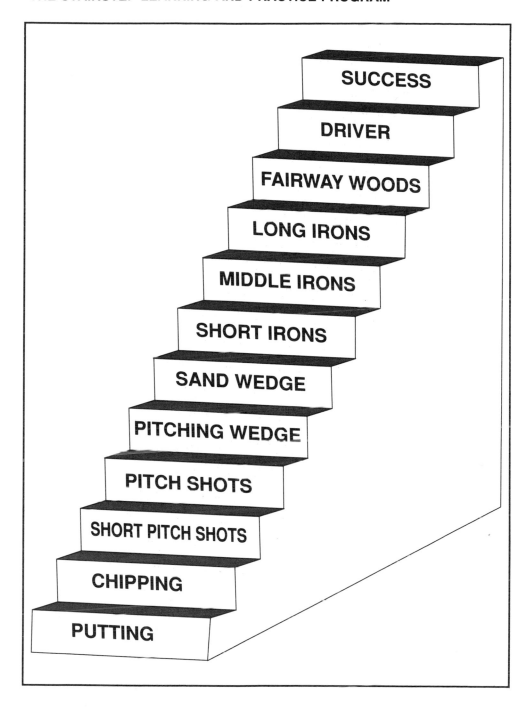

Step 1—Putting

My work in putting was set up on the 36-hole practice green at Jacaranda Country Club. Before each session, I would check my grip—the overlapping grip—and my stance. My feet are ten inches apart. My knees are flexed and I bend forward from the hips until my eyes are directly over the ball. I play the ball just off my left heel, placing my putter squarely behind the ball. I hit a few warm up putts, both long and short, and then I am ready to practice.

I start by placing balls in a circle two-and-one-half feet from the cup. I practice these putts until I drop them all perfectly. I then move the balls to ten feet from the hole and practice until all the balls drop into the hole.

I use the same technique to putt from twenty-five feet. I practice until I drop fifty percent and the rest come within six inches of the cup. I do the same from fifty feet, but I practice until all putts are within a one-foot circle around the hole. This is the way I practice on the green.

I move to the fringe and I line up the balls from the edge to thirty feet around the cup. I practice until I can drop the close putts and practice the longer putts until they stop one foot from the cup. I then move to a sand trap with no lip and practice putts from the sand until I can putt the balls to within one foot of the hole.

In all putts, I move the club with the triangle of the arms, shoulders and hands, keeping the grip just firm enough to have good control of the putter. I notice the contours of the green and how they will affect the movement of the ball. I putt to the high side of the cup so the ball will have a chance to fall, trying to put rhythm into the swing so that all putts are smooth. I practice this putting procedure for five days until I have mastered it. Only then do I move up to the next step on the stairway.

After each period on the practice green, I move to the driving range to work on shots beginning with the sand wedge. These are high lofting shots. I hit five balls at a time to land within a three-foot circle around the cup on the green. I use the Ultimate Golf Swing Fundamentals with each club listed in the stairstep program.

Step 2—Chipping

The putting grip can also be used for chip shots. The chip shot swing is a natural extension of the putting stroke. My chipping stance is slightly open and slightly more upright. My feet are five inches apart and my head higher. The ball is placed at the center of my stance. I use the 5, 6 and 7 irons for chip shots. My triangle moves the club back and through the ball. There is no wrist break in the chipping stroke and my left arm is kept straight. My right elbow is kept close to my right hip. I let the club lift the ball by using a slight descending stroke.

I practice chip shots at varying distances, from one hundred feet from the fairway on in to the pin. The ball should land on the green and roll to the cup. I practice until proficiency is such that only an uphill tap-in is left at the cup. I practice chip shots from the fringe and from sand traps with no lips. I practice all chip shots to enter the cup or have a six-inch tap-in. I allow for the way the contour of the green affects the ball. On the driving range, I am still working with pitch shots.

Step 3—Short Pitch Shots

For short pitch shots I use the Vardon, or overlapping, grip. My stance for the short pitch shot has knees flexed and hands ahead of the ball; my stance is open, with my feet ten inches apart. My weight is slightly on the target foot. The ball is played a little ahead of my rear heel. There is little body movement in short pitch shots. I use the pendulum swing and stroke the ball smoothly to the target. The backswing is shorter than the forward swing; my follow-through will be lower. I visualize the target before swinging, and think "target" when I swing.

I hit short pitch shots over bunkers, rough terrain or obstacles where a chip shot is not feasible. I consider the contour of the green and I practice all short pitch shots until a short uphill tap-in at the cup is left. The irons for these shots are the 7, 8 and 9 irons or wedge. I use the short pitch shot from the fairway fifty yards into the pin. A waist-high backswing will move the ball forty yards, while a one-third backswing will move the ball twenty-five yards with an 8 iron. The short irons are the clubs I use on the driving range. The short irons are as follows: sand wedge, pitching wedge, 9 iron and 8 iron.

Step 4—Pitch Shots

Pitch shots are high lofting shots made from one hundred yards down to fifty yards from the green. These shots are made with the 6, 7, 8 and 9 irons.

My motion in pitch shots relates to the motion of tossing a baseball underhand. My full backswing reaches just above my waist. My wrists hinge slightly and my weight shifts slightly to my target foot. My follow-through is somewhat longer than the backswing.

My stance is open, with feet ten inches apart; knees flexed; weight slightly on the target foot; my hands are ahead of the ball. My eyes are over the ball, which is placed ahead of the rear heel, toward the center of my stance.

My triangle moves the club back until the wrists start to cock, just past hip-high. My triangle is swung down on the same path and through the ball to my follow-through. I keep my hands ahead of the club head in the downswing. Keeping body movements to a minimum, I aim all pitch shots to the pin. I practice by hitting five balls at a time until I can place five in a cluster three feet from the cup.

Step 5—The Short Irons

Short irons are precision clubs for pitch shots, full shots, shots from rough, high grass, sand traps and fairway bunkers. A full swing three-quarters high is necessary to obtain the yardage listed below. My stance is open with feet ten inches apart. I play the ball at center between the feet. My hands are ahead of the ball and my weight is favoring the target foot. My knees are flexed and I bend forward from the hips.

My average distances with short irons are:

Sand wedge—75 yards
Pitching wedge—105 yards
9 iron—115 yards
8 iron—125 yards
7 iron—130 yards

In the backswing I move the triangle straight back from the ball past the right foot upward until my wrists cock just at shoulder-height. My club will point over my right shoulder toward the target. I start the downswing by turning my left hip to the left, which pulls the triangle down. My head stays behind the ball as my triangle moves into the impact area and down and through to a natural, high follow-through.

I hit five balls at a time with each short iron until I can land all five shots in a cluster three feet from the pin. I also practice fade and draw shots the same way. At each practice session preceding work on the driving range, I practice putting, chipping and short pitch shots. I am warmed up when I start practice on the driving range.

Step 6—The Middle Irons

My average distances with the middle irons are:

6 iron—140 yards
5 iron—155 yards
4 iron—165 yards

I use the middle irons for full shots from the fairway to the green. They are also used for long bunker shots. My swing with the middle iron is compact, the grip firm, the backswing short just to shoulder-height. The stance is more upright, as the length of the club dictates. My stance for the middle irons is open; my feet fourteen inches apart; weight on the target foot and hands ahead of the ball. The ball is played back from center of my stance. My knees are flexed and I bend forward from my hips.

The club must be swung smoothly, counting "one and two." The triangle moves straight back past the right foot and continues upward to a three-quarter backswing. The wrists cock naturally and the club points over the right shoulder toward the target.

I turn my hips to the left to begin the downswing. This also moves my hands and arms downward toward the waist and my weight transfers to the target leg. The triangle continues downward past the right knee into the hitting area. The left hand guides the club and the right hand smashes the ball at impact. My body position at impact is approximately the same as it was at address. The swing continues past impact on out toward the target. My right arm straightens and the left arm folds into a natural follow-through with the body facing the target.

I hit the middle irons by determining the distance for which I can use each club. I hit five balls at a time until I can hit them close together on the driving range. I do the same practice with each club. I also work on fading and drawing the ball.

Step 7—The Long Irons

My average distances with the long irons are:

3 iron—175 yards

2 iron—185 yards

The long irons are needed for long shots from the fairway. I make certain that the longer backswing and forward swing are rhythmic and smooth.

The swing with the long irons is a sweeping swing when the lie of the ball is good. Tight lies require a downward stroke striking the ball first and then taking the turf. My hands reach no higher than the top of the shoulder in the backswing. My stance for the long irons is square; my feet are eighteen inches apart; my weight is slightly on the target foot. My hands are slightly ahead of the ball which is placed four inches back from my target heel. My knees are flexed and I bend from the hips.

The swing with the long irons begins with the left arm straight and the right arm soft. I move the triangle back from the ball, past the rear foot, then continue upward to a full backswing with the wrists cocked above my shoulder level. My shoulders turn fully with my back to the target. The club will point over my right shoulder toward the target.

The downswing begins with my hips turning to the left. This drops the triangle toward the waist and begins the transfer of my weight to the target foot. The triangle continues into the hitting area, the left hand guiding and the right hand ready to smash the ball at impact. The swing is down and through the ball with turf taken after the hit. The swing continues through impact on out toward the target. My right arm straightens and the left arm folds into a natural follow-through with the body facing the target.

I hit long irons smoothly and with good timing, letting the club do the work. I hit the long irons on the driving range, hitting five balls at a time until I can land them close together on the range. I hit the same number of balls with each long iron club. I hit both fades and draws with the long irons. I swing long irons with the same force as I use with the middle irons. Rhythm and good timing result in good and easy shots.

Step 8—The Fairway Woods

The fairway woods and their distances are:

    5 wood—185 yards
    4 wood—200 yards
    3 wood—220 yards

I use the fairway woods for tee shots and for good lies on the fairway. I use the sweeping stroke from good lies and the downward stroke for tight lies. I use the 5 wood from the rough if the lie is good enough.

My stance with the fairway woods is square; feet twenty inches apart; weight slightly on the target foot. The ball is placed two inches back from my target heel. My hands are slightly ahead of the ball. My knees are flexed and I bend forward from the hips.

The swing begins with the left arm straight and the right arm soft. I move the triangle straight back from the ball past my rear foot and continue upward to a full backswing. My wrists have cocked naturally near the top of my head. The club points over my right shoulder toward the target. The downswing begins when I turn my hips to the left, which causes the triangle to drop toward my waist. My weight begins to transfer to the target foot. My body position stays steady as my triangle moves into the hitting area with the left hand guiding and the right hand ready to smash the ball at impact.

My swing is down and through the ball. The swing continues through impact; my right arm straightens and my left arm folds into a natural, high follow-through. The swing has rotated around my spine as my spine stays in exactly the same position throughout the swing.

For a good lie on the fairway, I use a sweeping stroke and for tight lies I use a downward stroke, taking turf after the ball is contacted. I practice fairway woods on the driving range. I hit five balls at a time until I can cluster them close together on the range. I practice straight shots first, then work the same way, perfecting fades and draws, with all the fairway woods.

Step 9—The Driver

Balance and relaxation are important in working with the driver. My stance is slightly closed with the feet shoulder width apart. The ball is placed one inch back from the target heel. My hands are slightly behind the ball; my knees are flexed and I bend forward from the hips until my arms hang free.

My backswing begins with my left arm straight and my right arm soft. I move the triangle straight back from the ball past the rear foot and continue upward to a full backswing with my wrists cocked naturally above my head. My shoulders turn fully with my back toward the target. The driver will point over my right shoulder at the target.

My downswing begins by turning my hips to the left, which drops the triangle toward my waist. My weight also begins to transfer to my target leg The swing continues as my triangle moves my hands and arms into the hitting area below my waist and onto impact with my left hand guiding and my right hand ready to smash the ball. My swing is down and through the ball into the follow-through. My right arm straightens and my left arm folds into a natural high follow-through. My driver contacts the ball slightly on the upswing.

I practice tee shots five balls at a time until I can cluster them close together on the range. I also practice fade and draw shots the same way. My average with the driver is 265 yards.

Step 10—Sand

I use two types of shots from bunkers and sand traps. The first is the pitch shot, which is easy to master. It is the same pitch shot practiced under step 4, "Pitch Shots." My explosion shot is made with the sand wedge.

My stance is slightly open; feet are shoulder width apart and dug into the sand. I play the ball one inch back from the target heel. I break my wrists quickly in the backswing; my grip pressure is firm. The club face is slightly open and I hit two inches behind the ball. I follow through with the palm of my left hand downward to keep the club face open during the swing. I practice each shot five balls at a time until I can land them one foot from the cup on the green.

Step 11—Playing Hilly Lies

Uphill—Level the stance by bending the left knee and play the ball back in the stance. Using a lower numbered club, swing slowly and smoothly, aiming to the right of the target.

Downhill—Level the stance by bending the right knee. Play the ball back in the stance and use a more lofted club, swinging slowly and smoothly, aiming to the left of the target.

Sidehill—Place the ball below the feet. Keep the weight back on your heels. Play the ball from the middle of the stance. Grip the club on the end and aim to the left of the target.

Sidehill—Place the ball above the feet. Shorten the grip and swinging slowly and smoothly, aim to the right of the target.

I practice all hilly lie shots five balls at a time, working until I land five near the pin.

As I worked up the stairsteps, my game continued to improve. On the driving range both the iron shots and the wood shots were nearly perfect. When my practice reached the long irons, I was already shooting scratch. What a wonderful day when I had my first par round. I was playing the longer east course at Jacaranda. My partner that day was a seventy-nine-year-old gentleman, Joe, and he hit the ball straight for 150 yards.

Joe scored well with his straight unerring shots. I had a habit of taking three practice swings with the driver, and on the 2nd hole Joe asked me why. I told him I thought I needed them and he said, "You swing like a pro. Have you ever noticed that the pros never take a practice swing?" I agreed to try just setting up, aiming and firing. I shot 72 that day, and Joe got a real kick out of my par, since he had helped me to get it. I never again scored above par 72.

When I finished work with the driver, I practiced on the driving range, hitting five balls with every club, starting with the wedge, followed by the short irons, middle irons, long irons, fairway woods and, lastly, the driver. Every time I hit all the clubs a crowd would gather to watch me hit. Near my last practice session at Jacaranda, the starter, Jay, came excitedly through the crowd and said, "John, I don't know what you did to your swing to hit shots like this. In all my days I have never seen any pro hit the ball better." I began to get inquiries and telephone calls and people began to ask me to write up the fundamentals and my practice procedure and give them a copy.

At the 19th hole one day, discussing how I dropped from a 28 handicap to scratch, several pros present said, "Why don't you put this into a book?" I would always answer, "Who would want to read what a duffer would write?" But I decided to write up the Ultimate Golf Swing Fundamentals and the Stairstep Learning and Practice Program, for I began to feel that, after all, they were something special.

I was on a vacation in Tennessee, when Robert, a nephew by marriage, challenged me to write a book. He was a fine teacher, but little did he know of the problems I would experience in putting together a book on so technical a subject as golf. During my years in business, however, I had done much technical writing on subjects far more complex than a golf swing, so I reluctantly accepted the challenge.

I had read that ninety percent of golfers play between 90 and 100 strokes a round and that they are always seeking ways to better their handicaps. So this would be a case of a duffer writing a book for duffers. Also, statistics say that many people who would like to play golf feel it is too expensive, both in equipment and in lessons to learn. My book would be for beginners also.

Reams of paper and six months later, I had a draft of *How I Went from 28 to Scratch in One Year Playing Once a Week at the Age of 70.* It was a golf instruction book truly worthy, I thought, to be the official teaching book for PGA pros. Ken Venturi recommended that I publish it, and hire a young pro on his way up on the tour to pose for the illustrations. I contacted the agents of several pros and finally selected a young pro. Paul Azinger had not yet won a tournament on the Pro Tour. He was playing in a tournament in Boca Raton and invited me to have lunch with him in the players' lunchroom. During lunch, he introduced me to several of the pros present. He and I spent three hours reading the manuscript. He was impressed and thought it would make a good book.

As we relaxed after reading the manuscript, I told Paul of my research for the Ultimate Golf Swing Fundamentals and the Stairstep Learning and Practice Program. I showed him several of my handicap cards, which reflected my scratch scores, including two rounds of 69. Here are the cards I showed Paul, who became very excited and said, "Man, this is fantastic."

GOLF HANDICAP CARD				HANDICAP
JOHN YOUNGBLOOD				7 *
PLANTATION GOLF CLUB				
February 12, 1985				99578

MOST RECENT SCORES FIRST, LEFT TO RIGHT					LOW SCORE DIFFERENTIAL
74<	77<	78<	76<	74<	7.1
76<	79	83	78<	76<	AVERAGE
77<	75<	78	83	79	LAST 20 AVERAGE
80	78	79	85	89	78.7

< INDICATES SCORES USED IN COMPUTATIONS	SCORES THIS CYCLE
GEO. LUMSDEN, P.G.A.	8

GOLF HANDICAP CARD				HANDICAP
JOHN YOUNGBLOOD				3
PLANTATION GOLF CLUB				
Jun 11, 1986				98400

MOST RECENT SCORES FIRST, LEFT TO RIGHT				LOW SCORE DIFFERENTIAL
72	72<	73	74	76	3.0

AVERAGE

LAST 20 AVERAGE 73.4

< INDICATES SCORES USED IN COMPUTATIONS	SCORES THIS CYCLE
BOBBY GOODMAN, P.G.A.	5/86

GOLF HANDICAP CARD				HANDICAP
JOHN YOUNGBLOOD				2 *
PLANTATION GOLF CLUB				
July 17, 1986				98400

MOST RECENT SCORES FIRST, LEFT TO RIGHT					LOW SCORE DIFFERENTIAL
72	72	71<	72	71	2.5
72	72<	72<	73	74	AVERAGE
76					LAST 20 AVERAGE 73.4

< INDICATES SCORES USED IN COMPUTATIONS	SCORES THIS CYCLE
BOBBY GOODMAN, P.G.A.	6

GOLF HANDICAP CARD				HANDICAP
JOHN YOUNGBLOOD				2
PLANTATION GOLF CLUB				
August 13, 1986				98400

MOST RECENT SCORES FIRST, LEFT TO RIGHT					LOW SCORE DIFFERENTIAL
70<	71<	72	72	71<	2.13
72	72	72	71<	72	AVERAGE
71<	72	72<	72<	73	LAST 20 AVERAGE
74	76				72.1

< INDICATES SCORES USED IN COMPUTATIONS	SCORES THIS CYCLE
BOBBY GOODMAN, P.G.A.	6

GOLF HANDICAP CARD				HANDICAP
JOHN YOUNGBLOOD				2
PLANTATION GOLF CLUB				
September 15, 1986				98400

MOST RECENT SCORES FIRST, LEFT TO RIGHT					LOW SCORE DIFFERENTIAL
72	71<	73	70<	72	2.0
71<	70<	71<	72	72	AVERAGE
71<	72	72	72	71<	LAST 20 AVERAGE
72	71<	72	72<	72<	71.6

< INDICATES SCORES USED IN COMPUTATIONS	SCORES THIS CYCLE
BOBBY GOODMAN, P.G.A.	6

GOLF HANDICAP CARD				HANDICAP
JOHN YOUNGBLOOD				1 *
PLANTATION GOLF CLUB				
October 20, 1986				98400

MOST RECENT SCORES FIRST, LEFT TO RIGHT					LOW SCORE DIFFERENTIAL
72	71<	70<	69<	71<	1.5
72	72	71<	73	70<	AVERAGE
72	71<	70<	71<	72	LAST 20 AVERAGE
72	71<	72	72	72	71.3

< INDICATES SCORES USED IN COMPUTATIONS	SCORES THIS CYCLE
BOBBY GOODMAN, P.G.A.	8

GOLF HANDICAP CARD					HANDICAP
JOHN YOUNGBLOOD					1
PLANTATION GOLF CLUB					
November 18, 1986					98400
MOST RECENT SCORES FIRST, LEFT TO RIGHT					LOW SCORE DIFFERENTIAL
72	72	70<	70<	69<	1.0
71	70<	72	71	70<	AVERAGE
69<	71	72	72	71<	LAST 20 AVERAGE
73	70<	72	71<	70<	70.9
< INDICATES SCORES USED IN COMPUTATIONS					SCORES THIS CYCLE
BOBBY GOODMAN, P.G.A.					7

GOLF HANDICAP CARD					HANDICAP
JOHN YOUNGBLOOD					1
PLANTATION GOLF CLUB					
December 16, 1986					98400
MOST RECENT SCORES FIRST, LEFT TO RIGHT					LOW SCORE DIFFERENTIAL
72	72	70<	70<	69<	1.0
71	70<	72	71	70<	AVERAGE
69<	71	72	72	71<	LAST 20 AVERAGE
73	70<	72	71<	70<	70.9
< INDICATES SCORES USED IN COMPUTATIONS					SCORES THIS CYCLE
BOBBY GOODMAN, P.G.A.					11/86

GOLF HANDICAP CARD					HANDICAP
JOHN YOUNGBLOOD					+1*
PLANTATION GOLF CLUB					
January 13, 1987					98400
MOST RECENT SCORES FIRST, LEFT TO RIGHT					LOW SCORE DIFFERENTIAL
71	69<	73	72	70<	+0.9
71	72	72	70<	70<	AVERAGE
69<	71	70<	72	71<	LAST 20 AVERAGE
70<	69<	71<	72	72	70.9
< INDICATES SCORES USED IN COMPUTATIONS					SCORES THIS CYCLE
BOBBY GOODMAN, P.G.A.					6

GOLF HANDICAP CARD					HANDICAP
JOHN YOUNGBLOOD					+1
PLANTATION GOLF CLUB					
February 23, 1987					98400
MOST RECENT SCORES FIRST, LEFT TO RIGHT					LOW SCORE DIFFERENTIAL
70<	70<	70<	69<	72	+0.6
71	70<	69<	73	69<	AVERAGE
72	70<	71	71	69<	LAST 20 AVERAGE
73	72	70<	71	72	70.7
< INDICATES SCORES USED IN COMPUTATIONS					SCORES THIS CYCLE
BOBBY GOODMAN, P.G.A.					13

Paul suggested that I write up my experiences with the Ultimate Golf Swing Fundamentals and the Stairstep Learning and Practice Program and add this to the manuscript.

I then showed Paul the computer printout from my handicap service, which listed my name as number one in the service.

Paul agreed that golfers with stalemated handicaps at 28 and above, and anyone who can read and has the desire to learn golf are suffcient market for this book. Paul agreed to pose for the photos to illustrate the Ultimate Golf Swing Fundamentals and we set up a date for the photo session. I arranged with Jerry Shelke of Rolling Hills Golf Club in Plantation, Florida to have the photo session on their course. The photos were to be shot by Tom Thurston of Apogee Photographers, Fort Lauderdale, Florida.

Rank	Diff	Hcp.	Player's name	Rank	Diff	Hcp.	Player's Name
1	+0.60	+0.6	YOUNGBLOOD, JOHN	41	19.8	19.0	GULLER, CARL
2	+0.30	+0.3	HALL, THURMAN	42	20.10	19.3	CAREY, FRANK
3	6.33	6.1	LESLIE, GEORGE	43	20.30	19.5	LYNCH, JACK
4	7.5	7.2	HAGLOF, RUSSELL	44	20.33	19.5	SCHECKTON, JOHN
5	8.29	8.0	POLLINGER, GEOR	45	20.43	19.6	MONGATO, JACK P.
6	8.70	8.4	HAGLOF, SUSAN	46	20.50	19.7	BRYAN, JAMES P.
7	9.67	9.3	MURPHY, BILL	47	20.67	19.8	PALMACCI, BOB
8	10.67	10.2	TRIFICANO, TERR	48	21.00	20.2	MC CRAY, RODGER
9	11.00	10.6	WILLIAMS, GEOR	49	21.00	20.2	LAIRD, JAY
10	11.10	10.7	BRITTLE, WALT	50	21.50	20.6	FOSSATI, JULES
11	11.20	10.8	BAUMAN, HARRY	51	21.80	20.9	ADAS, DAVID
12	12.00	11.5	KALO, DAUNE	52	22.00	21.1	SURPRENANT, DON
13	12.00	11.5	CUCCHIRO, TONY	53	22.30	21.4	VANSE, DENNY
14	12.40	11.9	MC CRAY, J.N.	54	22.30	21.4	CASEY, JIM
15	12.50	12.5	ARGENTINE, NICK	55	22.40	21.5	WINFIELD, ROY
16	12.70	12.7	PERRY, KEN	56	22.50	21.6	LUND, ART
17	13.70	13.2	VANGAS, CHAS	57	22.70	21.8	WUNSCH, ADAM
18	13.75	13.2	DUFFEK, PAUL	58	23.00	22.1	PESCE, JOE
19	13.80	13.2	NORMANDY, MIKE	59	23.00	22.1	DE SANTIS, JOE
20	14.00	13.4	LEWEY, DICK	60	23.17	22.2	RANDALL, JEFF
21	14.10	13.5	LEAVITT, STEVE	61	23.50	22.6	HAYWOOD, CURT A
22	14.60	14.0	THOMPSON, M.J.	62	23.80	22.8	MAY, LE ROY
23	14.70	14.1	SAIN, DON	63	24.40	23.4	FITZGERALD, CHA
24	15.10	14.5	TWERDOW, ARTHUR	64	24.60	23.6	WEISSING, LOUIS
25	15.14	14.5	STOVALL, DALE	65	25.00	24.0	OSTRANDER, J.W.
26	15.57	14.9	FRATONE, RICH	66	25.00	24.0	JOHNSON, JOHN
27	16.00	15.4	SINGER, JERRY	67	25.00	24.0	BATTAGLIA, SAL
28	17.00	16.3	RAU, DAVID	68	25.30	24.3	HAGBERG, DICK
29	17.33	16.6	HEATON, DON	69	25.50	24.5	CHILDERS, FRANK
30	17.40	16.7	WILSON, DELBERT	70	25.70	24.7	MARENOVICH, THO
31	17.80	17.1	HUNT, WM.	71	26.50	25.4	HAMMER, H.J.
32	17.87	17.2	DICKMEYER, JAME	72	27.00	25.9	KEPKE, JIM
33	18.40	17.7	RANDALL, RANDY	73	28.33	27.2	SULLIVAN, RICK
34	19.25	18.5	LUNSFORD, ROY	74	29.40	28.2	HILL, WHITEY
35	19.30	18.5	WHITE, JOHN	75	31.00	29.8	BLANTON, ED
36	19.30	18.5	AGELOFF, AL	76	37.90	36.4	BACILE, JOE
37	19.50	18.7	JOHNSON, ROBERT	77	39.33	37.8	BROWN, HELEN
38	19.50	18.7	DINDIA, PAUL	78	****	****	LANGE, ED
39	19.50	18.7	BATTAGLIA, ROSS	79	****	****	CUSMANO, ANTHONY
40	19.67	18.9	HERMSEN, JIM				

Serviced by: Computer Golf Service, 1700 S.W. 12th Avenue, Boca Raton, FL 33432 for Plantation Golf Club, 7050 W. Broward, Plantation, FL.

Paul did a superb job posing for the photos. He was extremely cooperative. It was a pleasure to work with a fine tour-playing pro. Paul liked the book so much that he wrote a foreword. I would like to make it crystal clear that Paul posed for the Ultimate Golf Swing Fundamentals which I developed, and not his personal swing fundamentals.

What am I doing these days? Playing golf! My scoring average is 70.6, which I am working to better. The Ultimate Golf Swing Fundamentals and the Stairstep Learning and Practice Program will help me accomplish this goal. It works for me and it can work for you!

1

GOLF: THE GAME

Golf is played on various courses, usually composed of nine or eighteen holes. There are also par 60 and pitch and putt courses. Par for eighteen holes is usually seventy-two strokes. The challenge of the game of golf is to move a golf ball from a starting tee, through a mowed fairway to a closely mowed green into a four-and-one-quarter-inch cup, in the least strokes possible. There will be various obstacles and hazards to impede the player's progress.

The course will have holes to be played in three, four or five strokes for par. The total strokes taken to complete the holes on a golf course is the total score. The player who scores less than his opponent wins the match. Many wagers have been won and lost in rounds of golf. It is a keenly competitive game. To receive the full benefits of this fascinating game requires a full knowledge of the golf strokes, etiquette, the rules of golf and how golf is played. The benefits will be in direct proportion to the results of your study, practice, learning and playing golf. Good luck in pursuing this quest.

A Brief History of Golf

The earliest form of golf was probably a game played by shepherds in ancient times, who used the crooks of their staffs to hit stones toward a wooden stake. Later, Roman citizens and soldiers played a game called "pagancia." This game was played with a bent stick and a ball made of feathers.

What we now know as golf developed in Scotland, where it was played since ancient times. It is still sometimes called "the royal and ancient game." James IV and James V and his daughter, Mary Stuart, played golf. The Royal and Ancient Club dates from 1840. Among the captains of the Royal and Ancient Club have been King Edward VII in 1863, Prince Leopold in 1876, King Edward VIII in 1922, King George VI in 1930 and George, Duke of Kent in 1937. Francis Ouimet was the first American captain in 1952.

The Royal and Ancient is the supreme authority on golf in Europe. In 1952, The Royal and Ancient and the United States Golf Association (USGA) agreed upon a uniform code. The only difference now is in the size of the ball. The British ball is 1.62 inches in diameter, while the USGA ball is 1.68 inches in diameter. Both weigh 1.62 ounces. The early British professionals include: Old Tom Morris, 1821-1908, who won the British Open four times and his son, Young Tom, who also won the British Open four times. Willie Park, Sr. won the British Open four times between 1860 and 1875. Jamie Anderson won the British Open three times between 1877 and 1879. William Campbell served most of his life as a pro at St. Andrew's until 1948. Bob Ferguson was a pro at Troon. He won the British Open three straight years, 1880-1882.

Some prominent twentieth century British golfers include: H. Vardon, who won the British Open six times. Vardon, J.H. Taylor and Scot J. Braid won the British Open sixteen times among them between 1894 and 1914. These golfers were known as the "Great Triumvirate" and were mainly responsible for the formation of the Professional Golfers Association.

Some prominent twentieth century United States golfers include: Walter J. Travis who won the United States Amateur in 1900, 1901 and 1903 and the British Amateur in 1904. Jerome Travers won the United States Amateur in 1907, 1908, 1912 and 1913 and the United States Open in 1913. He also won the United States Open in 1915. Francis Ouimet won the United States Open in 1913 and won the United States Amateur in 1914 and 1931. Chick Evans won both the United States Open and the United States National Amateur in 1916. Robert T. Jones, regarded as the greatest golfer of modern times, made his debut in the United States National Amateur in 1916 and played until his 1930 Grand Slam. Bobby Jones won the British

Open three times, the British Amateur once, the United States Open four times and the United States National Amateur five times. He played for the United States against Britain in the Walker Cup matches in 1922, 1924, 1926 and 1930. Lawson Little won both the United States National Amateur and the British Amateur in 1934. He repeated both wins in 1935. Little turned pro in 1936 and he won both the United States Open and the Canadian Open.

After the Jones era, great amateurs were scarce. Robert J. Sweeny, Frank Stranahan and Billy Joe Patton were the leading amateurs of the 1950s. A successful amateur career often serves as the foundation for a professional career and by this method the United States has produced more outstanding golfers than any other nation.

Some of the greatest United States professionals have been: Walter Hagen, Gene Sarazan, Tommy Armour, Byron Nelson, Ben Hogan, Sam Snead, Lloyd Mangrum, Cary Middlecoff, Jimmy Demaret, Lew Worsham, Jack Burke and Bob Toski. Many modern day golfers have earned over a million dollars from golf. Some of golf's millionaires include Jack Nicklaus, Tom Watson, Lee Trevino, Ray Floyd, Tom Weiskopf, Hale Irwin, Arnold Palmer, Johnny Miller, Billy Casper, Gary Player, Tom Kite, Hubert Green, Miller Barber, Gene Littler, Jerry Pate, Ben Crenshaw, Bruce Crampton, Lanny Watkins, Bruce Lietzke, J.C. Snead, Lou Graham, George Archer, Al Geiberger, Andy Bean, Bob Murphy, Don January, Dave Stockton, David Graham, Charles Coody, Dave Hill, John Mahaffy, Larry Nelson, Bill Rogers, Gil Morgan, Craig Stadler, Frank Beard, Jim Colbert, Julius Boros, Calvin Peete, Curtis Strange and Paul Azinger.

Setting Goals

The beginner's instruction program will create the basic skills needed to play golf for relaxation and pleasure —for the weekend golfer— beginners and seniors. Those who already consistently make low scores will find the advanced instruction program helpful in sharpening skills to participate in amateur tournaments. Diligent practice and playing in amateur tournaments and the regular achievement of sub-par scores may have you consider a pro career.

The golfer is an athlete, as in any sport, and a physical health program balanced between rest, exercise, proper diet and weight control can pay dividends in good golf and a longer life. Best wishes for the attainment of any goal for which you desire to strive, to the golfer for pleasure, the amateur and the professional. All are within your reach and the rewards are many and great, so pick your goal and go! Golf is for all ages.

Make Playing the Golf Course Fun

Don't rush when you arrive at the golf course. Allow time for your practice shots and practice putts. Check on the local rules and take time to study the map on the back of the score card showing the holes to be played. Also, dress comfortably for the day's weather.

On the tee, visualize the shot to be made and the spot where you expect it to land. Concentrate on this spot as you stroke the ball. Do not think about the people watching you make your shot.

How you place the ball on the tee will affect your shot. To plan a hook or draw when hitting from the tee, place the ball on the left side of the tee. If you plan to slice or fade the ball, place it on the right side of the tee. Also tee the ball on the right side of the tee when there are bunkers lining the right side of the fairway. Aim down the middle of the fairway. Also use the right side of the tee for shots to a green where the pin is placed left, and bunkers are in front.

On dogleg holes bending to the left, aim the ball to the right side of the fairway. On dogleg holes bending to the right, aim the ball to the left side of the fairway. Use two clubs more, when hitting into the wind, and two clubs less, when the wind is from behind you. After the drive, choose a fairway wood or an iron to reach the green for your next shot. Play errant shots back to the fairway, where a safe shot can be made. Always play away from trouble, and don't gamble on any shot.

Sharpen up the short shots, and keep your putting skills sharp. Get to know how the contours on the green affect the ball. Learn to read the grain of the green, and learn to identify the target spot to putt over in order to allow for the break, when the ball rolls toward the cup. Learn to judge the speed of putts. The short shots are the ones that separate a golfer from a duffer.

ETIQUETTE ON THE GOLF COURSE

Most importantly, there must be absolute silence on the tee. No one should move, talk or stand close to or directly behind the ball or the hole when a player is preparing to make his or her shot.

Do not make your shot until the players in front are safely out of range. If you should accidentally hit your ball in the direction of other golfers, yell "fore" to warn them.

The player with the "honor" (the player who is making his or her shot first) should play before his opponent tees his ball.

Players should play without unnecessary delays and those searching for a ball should allow other players coming up to pass them. If you signal other players to pass, you should not continue play until those players are safely out of range. If a group playing a match fails to keep its place on the course and falls more than one clean hole behind the players in front, it should allow the group following to pass. Players should leave the putting green as soon as the results of the hole have been determined.

Before leaving a bunker, a player should carefully fill in any holes he may have made and players should always see that any turf cut or displaced in the fairway is replaced and pressed down. Players should see that they or their caddies do no injury to the holes, either by standing too close to them when the ground is soft or by carelessly replacing the flagstick.

When a player incurs a penalty, he should let his opponent know as soon as possible.

Playing the Holes in Golf

USGA standard yardage for men is:

Par 3 hole—up to 251 yards
Par 4 hole—251 to 470 yards
Par 5 hole—471 yards and over

USGA standard yardage for women is:

Par 3 hole—up to 210 yards
Par 4 hole—211 to 400 yards
Par 5 hole—401 to 575 yards
Par 6 hole—576 yards and over

WHEN WATCHING A TOURNAMENT

When you attend a golf tournament, be courteous, and don't talk and stay behind the lines. Do not yell or run where it might affect play. When the gallery is large, kneel or sit so those behind you can see. Do not walk through bunkers, tees or greens and do not carry cameras. Pick a spot at the fairway or putting green where you can review the action or pick a favorite pro and follow his group.

When watching at the practice tee, take the opportunity to study the swings and the results when the pros are hitting their practice shots. Notice their smooth strokes. Note their posture, alignment, waggle, forward press, backswing, downswing and follow-through. Observe the pros carefully to pick out fundamentals which could benefit your swing and game. When viewing a match on television, observe the lessons and shots demonstrated. Watch the swings and the close-ups of the pros hitting. Relax and learn!

When playing a par 3 hole, tee the ball when hitting from the tee to the green. Hit the shot high enough to land on the green. On shorter par 3 holes, aim the shot to land the ball covering the flagstick. This will prevent the ball from falling short.

When playing a par 4 hole, aim the tee shot to land on the fairway in position to make an iron shot to the green. Try to hit the green in a spot for an uphill putt, and then sink the putt for a birdie or two putt for par.

When playing a par 5 hole, aim the tee shot to land in a position that will give the right angle for a fairway wood shot. The fairway wood should land in position for an easy iron shot to the green. Try to have an uphill putt, and sink it for a birdie or two putt for a par. When making any shot in golf, always try to hit the shot that will make the next shot easier.

Development of a Golf Career

I will assume that you are a beginner who has progressed solidly through the beginner's program:

> **Putting**—on the green, from the fringe and from the sand
>
> **Chipping**—from the fringe, from the fairway and from the sand
>
> **Short pitch shots**—from the fairway, over the bunkers and from the rough
>
> **Pitch shots**—from the fairway and from the rough
>
> **Short irons**—from the fairway and from the rough
>
> **Pitching wedge**—from the fairway and from the rough
>
> **Sand wedge**—from the sand, from the fairway and from the rough
>
> **Middle irons**—from the fairway and from the rough
>
> **Long irons**—from the fairway and from good lies in light rough
>
> **Fairway woods**—from the fairway and from good lies in light rough
>
> **Tee shots, driver and other woods**—from the tee to the fairway

Practice is the glue that holds the golf swing together. It is on the practice tee where swing skills are developed and honed with great intensity. Concentration is a vital part of practice. Learn to visualize all shots in both practice and play.

Make sure that your clubs are properly fitted. It is time now to assemble your permanent playing clubs. Well-fitted clubs are a must in golf. Your progress through the program, and diligent playing and practice should have you breaking 80 consistently. To further help your development as a golfer, I have included the advanced program.

The Advanced Program

The advanced program is:

Address for the drive
Backswing for the drive
Downswing with the driver
Follow-through with the driver
Angle of the back
Target golf
Sand traps
Explosion shot
Uneven lies in the sand
    Uphill lies
    Downhill lies
    Chip from the sand
    From fairway traps
Maintaining same address routine for all shots
Hitting all clubs
Hitting a deliberate slice
Hitting a deliberate hook

To reach a scratch handicap will require practice that is in direct proportion to playing better. The advanced program will bring refinements to your skills with all clubs and all shots, making scratch attainable.

Golf is a target game. Learn to manage the tee shot, for it sets up the way the hole is played. A properly positioned drive will make the next shot easier. Manage the fairway woods. They are the clubs for distance, and the correct execution of shots with the fairway woods is necessary for good scores in golf. Manage the iron shots. They are the finesse clubs. Accurate shots to the green with the irons are the precision part of the game of golf. Correct shots with the irons result in lower scores. Of such stuff is good golf made!

Keep a balanced program composed of playing, practice and tournament play. This will keep your skills sharply in focus. When your handicap drops toward scratch, plan to enter USGA amateur tournaments. A PGA pro can advise you of amateur tournament schedules. College can provide the opportunity to develop further as a golfer. The golf coach and the team competition can be of great benefit. The experience gained in college is often the foundation for a pro career.

In preparing for pro golf, I recommend that you select a PGA teaching pro to work with you throughout your career. He can help you sharpen your skills to be a winner on the Pro Tour. Whatever your goal, golf is played for relaxation and pleasure. This great game can be played throughout a lifetime.

A teen-ager can learn golf, through the many programs available for youth sponsored by the PGA and local country clubs. A teen's proficiency in amateur golf can earn him or her a college scholarship. Team golf competition in college can often qualify a golfer for a professional career, either on the Pro Tour or as a teaching pro.

The purpose of this book is to supply the knowledge needed to acquire and develop the skills to become a low-scoring amateur, and through the advanced program, to develop professional skill status. The beginner should select his or her ultimate goal and work and strive to achieve it. The knowledge is here. Use it well.

2

GOLF CLUBS AND EQUIPMENT

Golf is played with clubs specifically designed for the purpose of the shot. A complete set is composed of fourteen clubs.

Wood Clubs

Driver — used from the tee to the fairway

5 wood—used from the tee and fairway shots

4 wood—used from the tee and fairway shots

3 wood—used from the tee and fairway shots

Iron Clubs

9 iron—used for short shots to the pin

8 iron—used for short shots to the pin

7 iron—used for shots from fairway to the green

6 iron—used for shots from fairway to the green

5 iron—used for shots from fairway to the green

4 iron—used for shots from fairway to the green

3 iron—used for shots from fairway to the green

2 iron—used for shots from fairway to the green

1 iron—used from the tee and fairway shots

Pitching wedge—used for accurate pitch shots

Sand wedge—used for sand shots and pitch shots

Putter—used for putting on the green, from fringe and from sand

Fourteen clubs is the maximum allowed by the USGA rules. Golf balls and clubs are manufactured to rigid USGA specifications. Beginners may purchase a "short set," with fewer than fourteen clubs. Matching clubs can be added later, as needed. A "matched set" of golf clubs are manufactured so that when the clubs are soled at the address position, the cap ends of the shaft of each club will form a parallel line with the ground. This allows the same address position with each club, regardless of length. As the clubs grow shorter, the player's hands move closer to his body. A PGA professional can help a beginner to select proper, well-fitted clubs. Such clubs will pay dividends in good scoring, and it is a pleasure to hit with clubs fitted to one's own frame.

Along with clubs, the player will need the following: a golf bag, shoes, golf glove, tees, balls and score cards. Advanced players sometimes carry a 1 iron or an extra wedge. However, the fourteen club limit must be observed.

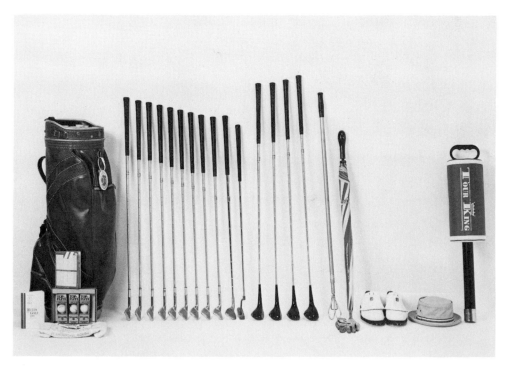

The full equipment for a golfer.

GOLF CLUB COMPONENTS

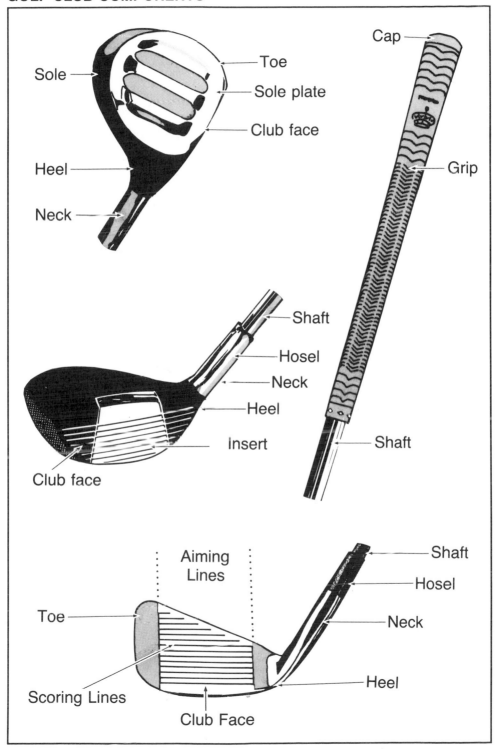

Iron clubs are made from forgings or castings of iron or stainless steel. Metal wood clubs have been developed recently, and graphite is now used in the club heads and shafts of woods. The majority of the shafts now in use are made of "lite" steel. Wood clubs may have heads made of graphite, persimmon, laminated maple or metal. Because some golfers feel that they can hit more easily with woods, manufacturers now offer complete sets composed of woods from one through fourteen. There is also now a trend to make special clubs and sets of clubs for seniors. New players should have their clubs fitted by a qualified PGA pro. Comfortable clubs are a must for good golf scores.

APPROXIMATE PROFILES OF SHOTS

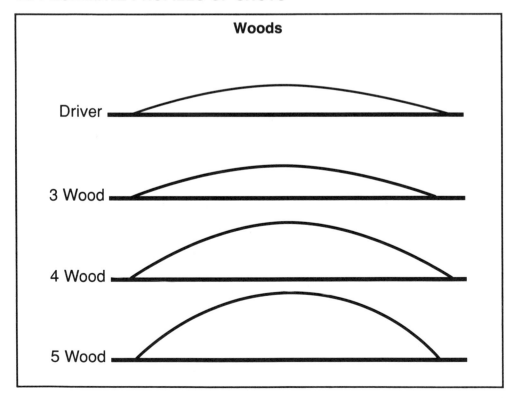

APPROXIMATE PROFILES OF SHOTS

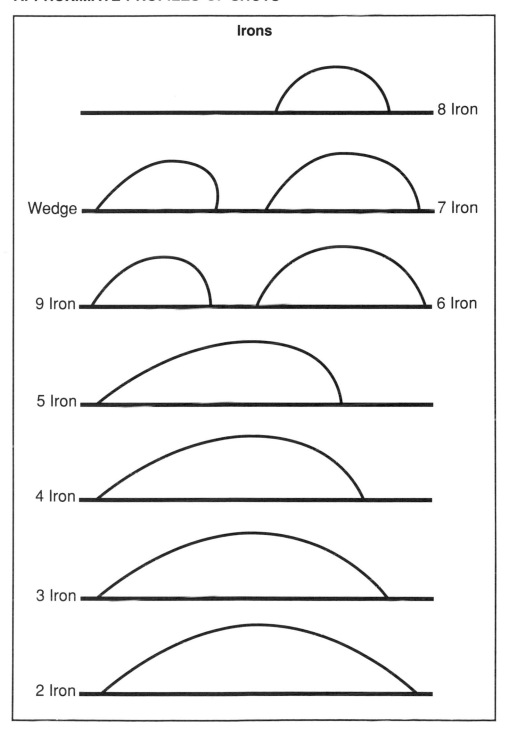

Golf Clubs and How They Relate to the Holes on a Golf Course

Par 3—Regulation: Tee shot to green, two putts into hole.

150 yards—Tee shot with a 5 iron. Chip and putt or just putt.
175 yards—Tee shot with a 3 iron. Chip and putt or just putt.
200 yards—Tee shot with a 4 wood. Chip and putt or just putt.
225 yards—Tee shot with a 3 wood. Chip and putt or just putt.
250 yards—Tee shot with a driver. Chip and putt or just putt.
275 yards—Tee shot with a driver. Short pitch shot with pitching wedge to green. Chip and putt or just putt.

Par 4—Regulation: Two shots to green, two putts into hole.

250 yards—Tee shot with a driver. Chip and putt or just putt.
275 yards—Tee shot with a driver. Short pitch shot with a pitching wedge to green. Chip and putt or just putt.
300 yards—Tee shot with a driver. Pitch shot with a pitching wedge to green. Chip and putt or just putt.
325 yards—Tee shot with a driver. Pitch shot with pitching wedge to green. Chip and putt or just putt.
350 yards—Tee shot with a driver. The 9 iron to green. Chip and putt or just putt.
375 yards—Tee shot with a driver. The 8 iron to green. Chip and putt or just putt.
400 yards—Tee shot with a driver. The 5 iron to green. Chip and putt or just putt.
425 yards—Tee shot with a driver. The 3 iron to green. Chip and putt or just putt.
450 yards—Tee shot with a driver. Second shot with a 4 wood to green. Chip and putt or just putt.

Par 5—Regulation: Three shots to green, two putts into hole.

401 yards—Tee shot with a driver. The 6 iron to the green. Chip and putt or just putt.

425 yards—Tee shot with a driver. The 3 iron to the green. Chip and putt or just putt.

450 yards—Tee shot with a driver. Second shot with a 3 wood to the green. Chip and putt or just putt.

475 yards—Tee shot with a driver. Second shot with a 3 wood to the green. Chip and putt or just putt.

500 yards—Tee shot with a driver. Second shot with a 3 wood. Short pitch shot with a sand wedge to the green. Chip and putt or just putt.

525 yards—Tee shot with a driver. Second shot with a 3 wood. Pitching wedge to the green. Chip and putt or just putt.

550 yards—Tee shot with a driver. Second shot with a 3 wood. The 9 iron to the green. Chip and putt or just putt.

575 yards—Tee shot with a driver. Second shot with a 3 wood. The 9 iron to the green. Chip and putt or just putt.

600 yards—Tee shot with a driver. Second shot with a 3 wood. The 7 iron to the green. Chip and putt or just putt.

The foregoing will be subject to variation as you play different courses and give consideration to tight driving holes and those with doglegs.

Golf's ever changing panorama of shots always tests the mettle of the player. He or she must play the shot that will make the next shot easier. The club selection must be correct and his swing coordinated and smooth to stroke the ball to the target. It is this variability that keeps golf the challenging game of a lifetime. Golf is a game of variables, and the skill to control them gives golf its fascination. Golf is a relaxing game, and must be played in a relaxed way for the best results. Golf is healthful, and the exercise of walking and swinging clubs is very beneficial.

GOLF CLUB AVERAGE SPECIFICATIONS

Club	Lie	Loft	Length
Driver	55°	11°	43¼"
5 wood	56°	22°	41¼"
4 wood	55¾°	19°	41¾"
3 wood	55½°	16°	42½"
9 iron	62°	46°	35½"
8 iron	61½°	42°	36"
7 iron	61°	38°	36½"
6 iron	60½°	34°	37"
5 iron	60°	30°	37½"
4 iron	58½°	26°	38"
3 iron	59°	23°	38½"
2 iron	58½°	20°	38½"
1 iron	58°	18°	39½"
Pitching wedge	63°	51°	35"
Sand iron	63°	57°	35"

GOLF CLUB AVERAGE YARDAGE

Irons	Yardage
Sand wedge	75 yards in to the pin
Pitching wedge	105 yards in to the pin
9 iron	115 yards in to the pin
8 iron	125 yards in to the pin
7 iron	135 yards in to the pin
6 iron	145 yards in to the pin
5 iron	155 yards in to the pin
4 iron	165 yards in to the pin
3 iron	175 yards in to the pin
2 iron	185 yards in to the pin
1 iron	195 yards in to the pin

Woods	Yardage
5 wood	185 yards; tee and fairway shots
4 wood	200 yards; tee and fairway shots
3 wood	220 yards; tee and fairway shots
1 wood (driver)	235 yards and up and tee shots

THE STAIRSTEP LEARNING AND PRACTICE PROGRAM

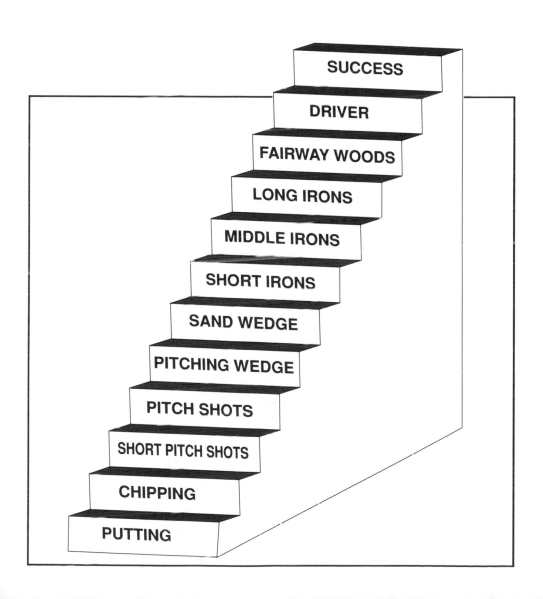

SUCCESS

DRIVER

FAIRWAY WOODS

LONG IRONS

MIDDLE IRONS

SHORT IRONS

SAND WEDGE

PITCHING WEDGE

PITCH SHOTS

SHORT PITCH SHOTS

CHIPPING

PUTTING

The learning program pictured is foolproof, provided that you become skilled in each step before continuing up the ladder. When you are skilled in putting, chipping is just an extension of the putting stroke. The skill attained at each step provides a solid foundation for the step above. Thus when you have finished working with the driver, you will be skilled in producing good shots with all clubs. You will then be ready to play golf. Follow the instructions for practice and be sure not to skip any steps on the stairway.

Remember, I used this program to rebuild my golf game, dropping my handicap from 28 to scratch. You too can do this. This program is for beginners, as well as for golfers of all ages who want to develop the skills to reduce their handicaps. Remember—climb the stairway step by step and achieve golfing success!

Golf for Beginners

A starter set of clubs composed of a driver, a 3 wood, a 9 iron, a 7 iron, a 5 iron, a 3 iron and a putter will be ample to learn the basic shots in golf. Matching clubs can be added to this short set later as needed.

We believe that golf is learned from the ground up and for that reason we begin our instruction with learning to putt.

Learning to Putt

Putting accounts for about fifty percent of the strokes in a round of golf. Therefore, it is important to know the fundamentals of putting and how the contours of the green affect the roll of the ball to the cup. Basic to all golf shots, including putting, is the need to have a good stance.

THE BASIC GOLF STANCE

The exercise below will teach you the basic golf stance. This stance will serve, with variations, as the basic address position for all golf shots.

1. Stand with the back against a wall, feet shoulder width apart.
2. Place the heels three inches from the wall.
3. Point the right foot straight ahead. Turn the left foot one-quarter turn to the left.

4. Place the back squarely against the wall, with the head touching the wall.
5. Flex the knees and slide the body one inch down the wall.
6. Bend forward, from the hips, shifting the weight to the balls of the feet.
7. Let the arms hang freely and lower the right shoulder, moving the right hand into a gripping position just inside the left leg.
8. Tap the heels, to make sure you are properly balanced.

Practice the foregoing set up for the stance until you can do it from memory and then practice it away from the wall. If your stance is correct, your legs will feel alert. The left arm should be straight and the right arm soft.

THE THREE BASIC STANCES

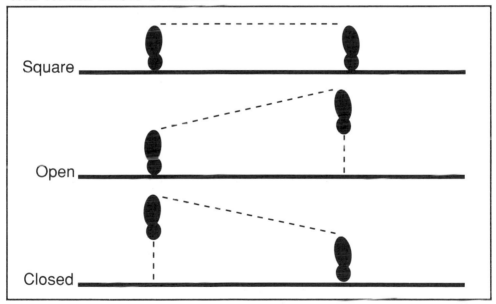

The square stance is used with the driver, fairway woods and long irons. Varying degrees of the open stance are used with the short irons and middle irons. Both the square stance and the closed stance are used for shots from the tee, with the driver, a 3 wood, a 4 wood or a 5 wood. The closed stance produces a slight hook, which gives more roll to the ball.

ADDRESS FOR THE PUTT

1. Assume the basic golf stance as in the exercise above.
2. Place the feet ten inches apart.
3. Center the weight between the feet.
4. Bend forward from the hips enough to bring the eyes directly over the ball.
5. Turn the left foot one-quarter turn to the left.

Imagine a line drawn from the target back through the ball. This line is called the "target line." Now imagine a line drawn from the ball straight back between the feet. This is called the "ball line." The left foot is called the "target foot" and the right foot is called the "rear foot."

For putting, we recommend the reverse overlap grip, used by most professionals. The left hand is placed at the top of the putter shaft, with the wrist straight and the thumb on top of the shaft. The shaft is gripped with the last three fingers of the left hand and the right hand is placed below the left, with all fingers on the shaft. The right thumb will also be on the top of the shaft. The index finger of the left hand should overlap the little finger of the right hand.

THE SWING FOR THE PUTT

When you have both stance and grip correct, place the head of the putter squarely behind the ball, aimed at the target. Note the inverted triangle formed by the shoulders, arms and hands. This triangle will be moved backward and forward with a slow, smooth rhythm. This triangle is used in all golf shots.

To feel the triangle rhythm, tie a string around a ball and swing it backward and forward. Note the rhythm and pace carefully, for this is the rhythm and pace for all future shots in golf.

When putting, only the arm and hands part of the triangle moves the putter. The putter is swung back slightly inside the target line and then swung forward, accelerating through the ball to the target. The ball will be played from a position just inside the target heel. Keep both the body and the head still for the best putting results. Make sure you are comfortable. Keep the arms close to the body and swing the putter with rhythm and pace. Count to yourself "one and two" or "back and through."

Putting can be practiced on the carpet at home by putting into a plastic glass. When you can make three shots out of every five, go to a practice green and notice how the contours and the grain of the grass affect your putts.

On the green, stand behind the ball and "read" the green by noting the grass. If the grass appears shiny, you will putt with the grain. If it has a dull appearance, you will putt against the grain. Notice the contours and allow for their influence on the ball. The putting stroke should be firmer in putting with the grain than against it.

Think about the distance to the cup and select a target spot over which to putt to correct the effects of contours on the ball. Now set up with your eyes over the ball and the putter squarely behind the ball and facing the target. Make sure your stance is comfortable and relaxed. Check your aim, stroke the ball to the target spot and listen for the "plop" as it drops into the cup.

Putts will have a chance to fall from the high side of the cup, but if they are on the low side, they can't. The low side is called the "amateur side." The putter can be used from the fringe around the green and also from shallow bunkers with low lips. When you use the putter from a trap, the ball should be sitting up from the sand. When you are dropping half of your putts, try putting from the fringe. When you can leave the putts close enough for a tap-in consistently, then try putting from a sand trap. Think of your goals and concentrate.

SUGGESTIONS FOR BETTER PUTTING

1. Assume the proper stance.
2. Take the proper grip.
3. Keep the shaft and the left arm in line. Aim square to the target.
4. Keep the forearms parallel to the target spot.
5. Focus the eyes over the ball. Feel the distance to the hole.
6. Hold the body still during the action.
7. Keep the putter low throughout the stroke.
8. Keep the head still.
9. Use a firm accelerating stroke.
10. Count "one and two," or "back and through." This will put rhythm into the stroke.

Putting stance on the green:

• Use the reverse overlap grip. Feet ten inches apart.
• Keep the eyes over the ball.
• Check both the "target line" and the "ball line."

Putting stance from the fringe:

• Keep the eyes over the ball.
• Maintain a comfortable stance.
• Hold the head still.
• Use a firm accelerating stroke.

Putting stance from sand:

• Keep the eyes over the ball.
• Hold the head still.
• Notice the triangle of arms and club.

Chip Shots

The reverse overlap putting grip can be also be used for chip shots. The chip shot is a natural gradation from the putt, for the stance is only slightly more upright, the head is higher and the ball closer to the feet. The eyes are in front of the ball. The inverted triangle of the shoulders, arms and hands form the pendulum stroke used for chipping and for all golf shots.

ADDRESS FOR THE CHIP SHOT

1. Take a slightly open stance, with the feet about five inches apart.
2. Center the ball between the feet.
3. Keep the left arm straight and the right elbow close to the right hip throughout the shot.
4. Weight should be slightly on the left foot.

THE SWING FOR THE CHIP SHOT

Use a straight lofted club, such as a 5 iron, for the chip shot. When swinging the club, the triangle moves the club back and through the ball. There is no wrist break in the chip shot stroke.

Swing as for a putt and let the club lift the ball by using a slightly descending stroke. The hands are ahead of the club head, and they stay ahead through impact and the follow-through. Keep the club low to the ground.

The chip shot is used for distances varying from one hundred feet from the fairway on in to the pin. The fairway must be free of bunkers. The ball should land on the green and roll to the cup. Practice the chip shot until proficiency is such that an uphill tap-in is all that is left after the shot. An example of a chip from twelve feet off the green would be to land the ball thirteen feet onto the green and have it roll forty feet to the pin. The length of your stroke and the force of the blow will determine the distance the chip shot will travel on the green to the hole.

SUGGESTIONS FOR BETTER CHIPPING

1. Hit chip shots smoothly, but firmly and crisply.
2. Play chip shots as long putts.
3. Keep the head and body still.
4. Choke down on the club if it provides better control.

5. Set the hands slightly ahead of the ball, at address, then pull the club head through the ball on the downswing with your hands leading.

6. Chip with different clubs, such as the 5 iron, the 7 iron and the 9 iron, according to the distance from the green.

7. Learn to hit the "soft" chip when the flag is near the front of the green. Use a 9 iron or a wedge and swing smoothly and firmly.

Chip shot backswing from the fairway: ▲

• Turn around a steady spine with the backswing.
• Use the triangle to move the club back and through the ball.

◄Chip shot stance from the fairway:

• Use the putting grip for chip shots.
• Place the feet five inches apart.
• Keep the eyes over the ball.
• Use the pendulum stroke for chip shots.

Chip shot follow-through from the fairway:

- Make sure there is no wrist break in the chip shot stroke.
- Keep the hands ahead of the club head. They stay ahead through impact and the follow-through.
- Keep the club low to the ground.

Chip shot stance for shots from the fringe:

• Keep the head and body still.
• Play chip shots as long putts.
• Hit chip shots smooth, but firm and crisp.

Chip shot backswing for shots from the fringe:

• Determine the distance the chip shot will travel on the green to the hole by the length of the stroke and the force of the blow.

Chip shot follow-through for shots from the fringe:

• Pull the club head through the ball on the downswing with the hands leading and through the follow-through.
• Chip with different clubs, such as the 5, the 7 and the 9 irons, according to the distance needed.

Chip shot stance for shots from the sand:

• Dig the feet into the sand to steady the stance.
• Notice the inverted triangle, evident in this picture.
• Choke down on the club if it provides better control.

Chip shot backswing for shots from the sand:

• The backswing turns around a steady spine.
• The length of the backswing and the force of the blow move the ball to the pin for a tap-in.

Chip shot follow-through for shots from the sand:

• Notice the head has not moved from the set up position.
• Make sure the triangle extends through impact and into the follow-
  through.

Short Pitch Shots

For short pitch shots we recommend the overlapping grip. This grip is used for all golf shots except putting, and is used by most golfers. Place your left hand on the grip below the cap. The back of the left hand faces the target. Close the hand with the thumb positioned slightly left of the shaft. Move the right hand over to the shaft, with the palm facing the target, with the fingers extended. Close the fingers around the shaft so that the little finger of the right hand overlaps the index finger of the left hand. Move the palm of the right hand to cover the left thumb. Keep the hands firmly together.

ADDRESS FOR THE SHORT PITCH SHOT
1. Place the feet about ten inches apart.
2. Flex the knees and put the weight slightly more on the target foot.
3. Place the ball a little ahead of the rear heel.
4. Straighten the arms and keep the right arm relaxed.
5. The straight left arm moves the club. The right arm remains relaxed until just before impact.

THE SWING FOR THE SHORT PITCH SHOT
There is little body movement in short pitch shots. Use a pendulum swing and stroke the ball smoothly to the target at which you have aimed. Take a shorter backswing and a longer forward swing than for the putt or chip shot. Accelerate crisply through the ball. Keep the head still and keep the weight on the left foot throughout the shot. The follow-through will be lower on this shot. Visualize your target before swinging and think "target" as you swing.

Short pitch shots are used over bunkers, rough terrain or obstacles where a chip shot is not feasible. When hitting short pitch shots, consider the contour of the green and try to approach the pin to leave a short uphill tap-in.

Practice the short pitch shot until you can consistently place it near the pin. Use a lofted club, such as the 7 iron, the 8 iron, the 9 iron or the wedge. This shot will stop quickly and will not run like a chip shot.

SUGGESTIONS FOR BETTER SHORT PITCH SHOTS

1. Be accurate and your short pitch shots will make it to the green.
2. Keep the left arm extended until the ball is well on its way.
3. Finish short pitch shots with the club face facing up toward the sky. Keep the left wrist firm, and facing the target at the finish.
4. Hit down on the ball and contact the ball first, then the turf.
5. Practice by lining up three balls in a row, ten inches apart. Try to land each ball at the same spot.
6. Plan the shot to cover all levels of the green. Make sure the selected club and the swing will produce the shot to reach the target.
7. Keep the shoulders parallel to the target line, when opening the stance.
8. Hit crisply through the ball. Do not swing "at the ball," or decelerate during the forward swing.
9. Play the pitch-and-run shot with a 7 iron or 8 iron. The stroke produces a lower shot which will run on the green.
10. Use the short pitch and the pitch-and-run shots from the fairway, fifty yards into the green.
11. Use a waist-high backswing to move the ball forty to fifty yards.
12. Use a one-third swing to move the ball twenty to forty yards.
13. Practice short pitch and pitch-and-run shots from various distances from the green.
14. Swing the arms freely and smoothly for the short pitch shot. Develop rhythm by using a light grip pressure. Keep the same grip pressure throughout the stroke. Never hurry the shot. The ball, on this shot, goes softly through the air and settles gently on the green.

Stance for short pitch shots from the fairway:

• Use the overlapping grip.
• Assume an open stance. The feet are ten inches apart.
• Keep weight slightly on the target foot.
• Place the ball a little ahead of the rear heel.
• Flex the knees.
• Use the pendulum swing.

Backswing for short pitch shots from the fairway:

• Take a shorter backswing and a longer forward swing.
• Accelerate crisply through the ball. Keep the head still.

Follow-through for short pitch shots from the fairway:

- Visualize the target before swinging and think "target" when you swing.
- Remember that there is little body movement in short pitch shot swings.

Stance for short pitch shots from the fringe:

- Assume an open stance. Feet are ten inches apart.
- Keep the hands firmly together.
- Use the straight left arm to move the club. The right arm is relaxed until just before impact.

Backswing for short pitch shots from the fringe:

• Use the pendulum swing and stroke the ball smoothly to the target.

Follow-through for short pitch shots from the fringe:

• Notice the follow-through is lower on this shot.
• Use short pitch shots over bunkers and rough terrain.

Stance for short pitch shots over the sand:

• Assume an open stance. Feet are ten inches apart.
• Flex the knees.
• Place the hands ahead of the ball.
• Bend forward from the hips until the eyes are over the ball.

Backswing for short pitch shots over the sand:

• Use a backswing waist-high to move the ball forty to fifty yards and a one-third swing to move the ball twenty to forty yards.

Follow-through for short pitch shots over the sand:

• Do not swing "at the ball" or decelerate during the forward swing, but hit crisply through the ball.

Pitch Shots

Pitch shots are made from one hundred yards down to fifty yards from the green. Pitch shots are made with the 6 iron, the 7 iron, the 8 iron and the 9 iron. The pitching wedge and the sand wedge can also be used. The motion in the pitch shots relates to the underhand motion in tossing a baseball.

Pitch shots are high lofting shots. The full backswing reaches just above the waist. The wrists hinge slightly and there is a slight degree of weight shift to the right foot. The follow-through is somewhat longer than the backswing.

Pitch shots may be hit by gripping down on the shaft an inch or two from the cap of the shaft to provide steadier control of the club.

ADDRESS FOR THE PITCH SHOT

1. Assume the open stance. Feet should be ten inches apart.
2. Keep the knees slightly flexed.
3. Weight should be slightly on the target foot.
4. Place the hands ahead of the ball.
5. Keep the eyes over the ball.
6. Keep the ball ahead of the right heel, toward the center of the stance.
7. Bend forward from the hips until the arms hang free.
8. Play the ball fairly close to the feet. Swing back slowly, keeping the right elbow close to the body.

THE SWING FOR THE PITCH SHOT

The swing moves the triangle of the shoulders, arms and hands, as a pendulum, back until the wrists start to cock. There is a slight shift of the weight to the right foot in the full backswing, which reaches just past the hips. The triangle is swung down on the same path, returning to the address position at impact and then through the ball into the follow-through. The weight transfers to the left leg on the down-swing. The hands stay ahead of the club head through impact.

Body movements are minimized in the pitch shot. Aim pitch shots to land on the green, near the pin. Practice pitch shots from varying distances from one hundred yards to fifty yards from the green.

SUGGESTIONS FOR BETTER PITCH SHOTS

1. Swing with light grip pressure.
2. Swing back to just above the waist to allow the weight to transfer to the right foot.
3. Use a descending stroke.
4. Be careful in opening the stance and keep the shoulders parallel to the target line.
5. Swing through the ball. Don't swing "at the ball."
6. Let the club head lift the ball. Do not "scoop" or lift the hands.
7. Count "one and two" when swinging to improve timing and rhythm.
8. Hit crisply and firmly, and follow through.
9. Control the length of the shot by the length of the backswing and the follow-through.
10. Control balance throughout the full swing. This is a must in all golf shots.
11. Use the pitch-and-run shot, if the green is hard and dry, because a pitch shot won't bite.
12. Close the club face slightly to cause the ball to roll more on the green, when playing the pitch-and-run shot from the one hundred foot area.
13. Aim pitch shots at the top of the flagstick. This prevents shots that are short of the green.
14. Play the high fade pitch shot with the shoulders, hips and feet aligned slightly to the left of the target line. Make sure the club faces the target. Play the ball opposite the target heel. Do not let the right hand cross the left during or just after impact. Use this slightly cut shot to produce a floating fade, dropping on the green.

Stance for pitch shots from the fairway:

• Assume an open stance. Feet are ten inches apart.
• Flex the knees slightly.
• Weight should be slightly on the target foot.
• Place the hands ahead of the ball.
• Keep the eyes over the ball.
• Place the ball ahead of right heel, toward the center of the stance.
• Bend forward from the hips.

One-quarter backswing for pitch shots from the fairway:

• The swing moves the triangle of the shoulders, arms and hands as a
  pendulum, back one-quarter and kept in a straight line with the club.

One-half backswing (full) for pitch shots from the fairway:

• The swing moves the triangle back, until the wrists start to cock. The full backswing reaches just past hip-high.

One-quarter downswing for pitch shots from the fairway:

• The swing is made around a steady spine.
• Keep the right knee in the same position and flex throughout the swing.

Impact for pitch shots from the fairway:

• Transfer the weight to the left leg in the downswing.
• Keep the hands ahead of the club head through impact.

One-half follow-through for pitch shots from the fairway:

• Minimize body movements in the pitch shot. Aim pitch shots to land on the green, near the pin.

Three-quarter (full) follow-through for pitch shots from the fairway:

• Swing with a light grip pressure.
• Swing through the ball. Don't swing "at the ball."
• Let the club head lift the ball. Don't "scoop" or lift the hands.

Stance for downhill pitch shot from the fairway:

• Bend the right knee to attain a level stance.

PLAYING FROM HILLY LIES

Uphill

Level the stance by bending the left knee. Use a lower numbered club and play the ball back in the stance. Aim to the right of the target. Lean slightly forward to maintain balance. Swing slow and smooth.

Downhill

Level the stance by bending the right knee. Use the open stance. Use a more lofted club. Play the ball back in the stance. Aim to the left of the target. Swing slow and smooth.

Sidehill

Keep ball below the feet. Keep the weight back on the heels. Grip the club on the end. Play the ball from the middle of the stance. Aim to the left of the target.

Sidehill

Keep ball above the feet. Shorten the grip and shorten the swing. Swing slow and smooth. Aim to the right of the target.

Stance for uphill pitch shot from the fairway:

• Assume an open stance. Feet are ten inches apart.
• Place the ball near the target heel.
• Hold the head behind the ball.

The Short Irons

The short irons and the average distances to the pin are:

Sand wedge—75 yards
Pitching wedge—105 yards
9 iron—115 yards
8 iron—125 yards
7 iron—135 yards

Short irons can be used for pitch shots, shots from the rough, high grass, sand traps and fairway bunkers. A full swing, with the back-swing to shoulder-height for the hands, is required to attain the yardage listed above. The full swing for a short iron shot is a three-quarter swing, which is recommended for all iron shots in the learning period for beginning players.

When practicing short iron shots, start with the pitching wedge and hit shots to a green fifty yards away. Practice at a practice green or a driving range. Hit shots until you can land ten in a row on the green and continue until five shots out of ten land within ten feet of the pin.

When you have reached proficiency with the wedge shots, set up practice sessions with the 9 iron, the 8 iron and the 7 iron. Hit these shots directly over the same green used with the wedge, to the full distance with each iron. Accurate approach shots with the short irons is vital to low scoring in the game of golf.

ADDRESS FOR SHORT IRON SHOTS
1. Assume an open stance. Keep the feet ten inches apart.
2. Turn the target foot left one-quarter.
3. Play the ball from the center between the feet.
4. Keep the hips and shoulders square with the target line when moving the left foot back in opening the stance.
5. Favor the weight on the target foot.
6. Keep the hands well ahead of the ball.
7. Flex the knees.
8. Bend forward from the hips.
9. Grip the club firmly for short iron shots.
10. Relax and make sure the stance is comfortable.

THE SWING WITH THE SHORT IRONS

When beginning the backswing, make certain that you take a level turn around your spine, without swaying, dipping or changing the angle of the back, shoulders or hips. Keep the head steady and move the triangle straight back from the ball past the rear foot. Keeping the left arm straight, turn the triangle around the spine to a full backswing just shoulder high. The wrists will cock naturally and the back will face the target. The hips will turn less than the shoulders. The club will point over the right shoulder toward the target.

The downswing begins by turning the left hip to the left, which pulls the hands down. The right elbow is close to the right hip and the hands continue down into the hitting area below the waist. The weight begins on the left foot and stays there throughout the shot. The head stays behind the ball and at impact the right hand hits down and through the ball, with the left hand guiding the club. The hit is made with the hands leading the club head and the swing continues to a high follow-through.

SUGGESTIONS FOR BETTER SHORT IRON SHOTS

1. Hit down, contacting the ball first, then take turf by hitting through the ball. Don't quit on short iron shots.

2. Do not "swing at," or try to "scoop" the ball.

3. Do not stand too far from the ball, so that reaching for the ball is necessary. Also, do not stand too close.

4. Choke the club shaft an inch or two if the shot feels more comfortable.

5. Make certain that the club face covers the ball on the backswing.

6. Keep the left arm fully extended until the ball is well on its way, for accuracy in short iron shots. Also, keep the wrists firm.

7. Hit a high fade, by playing the ball up near the target heel with the weight slightly on the target foot. Be sure that the right hand does not turn over after impact.

8. Keep the weight on the target foot throughout the swing for a low shot. Play the ball back past the center of the stance. Swing the club head downward into the turf after impact. Use a lower numbered club for longer shots.

Stance for short iron shots from the fairway:

• Assume an open stance. Feet are ten inches apart. Target foot is turned left one-quarter.
• Play the ball centered between the feet.
• Weight should slightly favor the target foot.
• Hold the hands ahead of the ball.
• Flex the knees.
• Bend forward from the hips.

One-quarter backswing for short iron shots from the fairway:

• Make a level turn around your spine, without swaying or dipping or changing the angle of the back, shoulders and hips.

One-half backswing for short iron shots from the fairway:

• Keep the head steady and move the triangle straight back from the ball past the right foot. Keep the left arm straight, turn the triangle back one half as shown.

Three-quarter (full) backswing for short iron shots from the fairway. A full backswing is just shoulder-high:

- The wrists cock naturally.
- The back will face the target.
- Turn the hips less than the shoulders are turned.
- Point the club over the right shoulder toward the target.

One-half downswing for short iron shots from the fairway:

• Begin the downswing by turning the left hip to the left which pulls the hands down.
• Keep the right elbow close to the right hip.
• Be sure your head is behind the ball.

Three-quarters downswing for short iron shots from the fairway:

• Weight is on the left foot and stays there throughout the shot.
• Make sure the hands are entering the hitting area below the waist, as shown above.

Impact for short iron shots from the fairway:

• The right hand hits down and through the ball, with the left hand guiding the club.
• Hit with the hands leading the club head.

One-half follow-through for short iron shots from the fairway:

- Don't quit on short iron shots. Hit down, contacting the ball first, then taking turf by hitting through the ball.
- Keep the left arm fully extended until the ball is well on its way, for accuracy on short iron shots.

Three-quarter follow-through for short iron shots from the fairway:

• Hit with the hands leading the club head. The swing continues to a high follow-through in perfect balance.

Full follow-through for short iron shots from the fairway:

• The swing continues through impact and out toward the target, the right arm now straightening and the left arm folding into a high follow-through.

The Middle Irons

The middle irons and the average distances with these clubs are:

6 Iron—145 yards
5 Iron—155 yards
4 Iron—165 yards

The middle irons are used for full shots from the fairway to the green. They are also used for long bunker shots. When hitting the green with a middle iron, stay with the shot through the follow-through. Don't quit on the shot or look up too soon. The swing with the middle iron is compact, the grip firm and the backswing short. The stance is more upright, as the length of the club dictates.

ADDRESS FOR THE MIDDLE IRONS

1. Assume an open stance. Keep the feet fourteen inches apart.
2. Place weight on the target foot.
3. Position the hands ahead of the ball.
4. Play the ball back toward the center of the stance.
5. Take the proper grip.
6. Flex the knees.
7. Bend forward from the hips.
8. Relax and keep the head still.

THE SWING WITH THE MIDDLE IRONS

With the left arm straight and dominant and the right arm soft, move the triangle of the shoulders, arms and hands straight back from the ball past the right foot and continue upward to a three-quarter backswing. The shoulders will turn fully with the back to the target and the hips will turn less. The club will point over the right shoulder toward the target. There will be some natural cocking of the wrists. Swing the club smoothly to the top of the backswing counting "one and two" or "back and through." Counting should be used in all shots, including putts.

The downswing begins by turning the hips to the left, causing the weight to begin transferring to the target leg. This drops the triangle toward the waist and on toward the right knee and right foot as the hands and arms move into the hitting area. The body stays steady and the triangle swings into the impact area with the left arm guiding and the right hand ready to smash the ball. The body position at impact is approximately the same as an address.

The swing continues through impact and on toward the target, the right arm straightening and the left arm folding into a natural follow-through. This swing will have been done around the spine. The address posture stays the same throughout the swing. As the triangle moves down toward the waist in the downswing, the right shoulder moves down and under while the hands move toward impact and the follow-through.

SUGGESTIONS FOR BETTER MIDDLE IRON SHOTS

1. Practice the middle iron clubs by determining the distance you can hit with each club. Hit with a smooth and easy swing.

2. Practice by hitting five balls at a time until you can hit them the same distance and to the same spot. Do this with each club. Record your distance.

3. Be sure the club you select will clear the lip when hitting from fairway bunkers.

4. Hit middle irons so that the club face contacts the ball first, before contacting the turf. The shot will fail if this is not accomplished correctly.

5. Be certain that the hands lead the club head when swinging middle irons through impact.

6. Stand the right distance from the ball. Do not reach or stand too close.

7. Grip the club firmly and make the backswing somewhat steeper and more upright when hitting from heavy grass. Make the downswing firm and sharp. Try to contact the ball before the heavy grass.

8. Hit only straight shots until you complete the beginner's instruction section. Curving shots will be covered in the advanced instruction section.

Stance for middle iron shots from the fairway:

• Assume an open stance. Feet are fourteen inches apart.
• Weight should be on the target foot.
• Play the ball toward the center of the stance.
• Keep the hands ahead of the ball.
• Flex the knees.
• Bend forward from the hips.
• Relax and keep the head still.

One-quarter backswing for middle iron shots from the fairway:

• Turn around the spine and move the triangle to the one-quarter backswing position.
• Keep the left arm straight.

One-half backswing for middle iron shots from the fairway:

• The swing continues upward until the club is parallel with the ground.
• Point the left knee behind the ball.

Three-quarter (full) backswing for middle iron shots from the fairway:

• Turn the shoulders fully with the back to the target and the hips will turn less.
• Point the club over the right shoulder toward the target.

One-half downswing for middle iron shots from the fairway:

• Begin the downswing by turning the hips to the left, causing the weight to transfer to the target leg. This drops the triangle toward the waist.

Three-quarter downswing for middle iron shots from the fairway:

• Keep the body steady as the arms and hands move into the hitting area, with the right hand ready to smash the ball.

Impact for middle iron shots from the fairway:

• Keep the body position at impact approximately the same as at address.

One-half follow-through for middle iron shots from the fairway:

• The swing continues through impact on out toward the target, the right arm now straightening in the one-half follow-through.

Three-quarter follow-through for middle iron shots from the fairway:

• Fold the left arm into a natural follow-through.
• The swing is around the spine.

Full follow-through for middle iron shots from the fairway:

• Face the target with the body in a natural, comfortable follow-
through.

The Long Irons

The long irons and their average distances are:

    3 Iron—175 yards
    2 Iron—185 yards

The long irons are used in long shots from the fairway. When hitting for the green, make certain that the longer backswing and the forward swing are rhythmic and smooth. The swing with the long irons is more sweeping, similar to sweeping shots with the fairway wood from a good lie. But if the lie is tight, the stroke must be downward, striking the ball first and then the turf. In the backswing, the hands should reach no higher than the back of the shoulder.

ADDRESS FOR THE LONG IRON SHOT

1. Assume a square stance. Keep the feet eighteen inches apart.
2. Place weight slightly on the target foot.
3. Position the hands slightly ahead of the ball.
4. Place the ball four inches back from the target heel.
5. Flex the knees.
6. Bend forward from the hips, not the waist.
7. Relax and keep the head still.
8. Keep the body comfortably erect.

THE SWING WITH THE LONG IRON

With the left arm straight and the right arm soft, move the triangle of the shoulders, arms and hands back from the ball past the rear foot, then continue upward to a full backswing, with the wrists cocked just above shoulder level. The shoulders will turn fully, so the player's back is to the target. The hips will turn less. The club will point over the right shoulder toward the target.

The downswing begins by turning the hips to the left, which causes the weight to begin transferring to the target leg, which also drops the triangle toward the waist and toward the right knee and right foot as the hands and arms move into the hitting area. The body stays steady and the triangle swings into the impact area with the left arm guiding and the right hand ready to smash the ball. The swing is down and through the ball. The ball is contacted first and turf taken after, but not as much turf is taken as for the middle irons. The body position at impact is approximately the same as it was at address.

The swing continues through impact and on toward the target, the right arm straightening and the left arm folding into a natural follow-through facing the target. The swing has been done around the spine. The posture at address stays the same throughout the swing. As the triangle moves downward toward the waist in the downswing, the right shoulder moves down and under, as the triangle moves toward impact and follow-through.

SUGGESTIONS FOR BETTER LONG IRON SHOTS

1. Take a full shoulder turn on the backswing.
2. Let the club do the work, don't force the shot. Hit smoothly and with good timing.
3. Let the loft and the length of the club shaft take care of distance. Trust the club to do this.
4. Be certain that the club head is swinging down at impact, so that turf is taken in front of the ball after the ball is hit.
5. Let the one-piece swing move the shoulders, arms, hands and hips all at the same time on the backswing and the downswing.
6. Make the stance comfortable at address and keep the head and body in the same relative position throughout the swing.
7. Play the ball four inches back from the target heel when hitting from a good lie. Take a smooth swing and aim at the green.
8. Play the ball further back, from a cupped lie and swing firmly down through impact.
9. Keep the arms close at address. Keep the right elbow close to the right hip in the backswing. Keep the arms close together in the downswing and the follow-through.
10. Swing the long irons with the same force as the middle irons. They do not require a harder swing.
11. Practice long iron shots by aiming shots to land at the same spot.
12. Concentrate on these swing reminders: "back and through," "back and shift," "stretch and spring," "one and two," "one and two, wait three," "back and smooth."

PLAYING FROM THE ROUGH

Grip the club firmly. Make the backswing somewhat steeper and make the downswing firm and sharp. Try to contact the ball before the rough. Keep the head steady.

PLAYING INTO THE WIND

Use two clubs longer than usual. Keep the ball low. Estimate the effect of the wind on the shot.

PLAYING WITH THE WIND

Keep the body steady. Do not sway or hurry the shot. Hit firmly and solidly—the ball will lose some spin and roll more.

CROSS WINDS

Estimate the effect of the wind on the shot. Correct the shot to have the wind bring the ball back into the intended target line.

PLAYING FROM SAND

Use the pitch shot swing. Open the stance with the feet worked into the sand. Hit behind the ball three inches. Swing low and smooth and into a full follow-through.

Stance for long iron shots from the fairway:

• Assume a square stance. Feet are eighteen inches apart.
• Keep the hands slightly ahead of the ball.
• Place the ball four inches back from target heel.
• Flex the knees.
• Bend forward from the hips.
• Keep the body comfortably erect.

One-quarter backswing for long iron shots from the fairway:

• Straighten the left arm, keep the right arm soft and move the triangle
  back to the one-quarter backswing position.

One-half backswing for long iron shots from the fairway:

• The body turns around a steady spine. The swing moves upward to the one-half position.

Three-quarter backswing (full) for long iron shots from the fairway:

• The swing continues to a full backswing, the wrists cocked just above
  shoulder level.
• Point the club over the right shoulder toward the target.

One-half downswing for long iron shots from the fairway:

• Begin the downswing by turning the hips to the left. This causes the weight to transfer to the target foot, and the hands and arms move downward.

Three-quarter downswing for long iron shots from the fairway:

• Move the hands and arms into the hitting area, the left arm guiding and the right hand ready to smash the ball.

Impact for long iron shots from the fairway:

- The swing continues through impact on out toward the target.
- Contact the ball first, turf taken after, but take less than for middle iron shots.

One-half follow-through for long iron shots from the fairway:

• As the triangle moves downward in the downswing, and as the right shoulder moves down and under, the triangle moves toward impact and the follow-through.

Three-quarter follow-through for long shots from the fairway:

• The swing has been made around the spine, as the posture at address stays the same throughout the swing.

Full follow-through for long iron shots from the fairway:

• The swing continues through impact on out toward the target, into a natural and comfortable follow-through.

The Fairway Woods

The fairway woods and their distances are as follows:

5 wood—185 yards
4 wood—200 yards
3 wood—225 yards

Fairway woods can be used for tee shots and good lies in the fairway and good lies in the rough. They may be hit from fairway bunkers, if the ball is sitting up and the lip is not too high for the shot to clear. The ball should be picked clean from the sand.

When hitting a 3 wood from the fairway from a good lie, hit with a sweeping stroke, and do not take turf. The swing is much like the swing you will learn to use with the driver.

Tight lies should be hit slightly on the downswing, nipping the ball first, and taking a little turf. Lies in the rough must be hit firmly downward. The 4 wood can be used from any lie, using the sweeping stroke for good lies and hitting downward on all others. The 4 wood can also be hit from the tee.

The 5 wood can be hit from the tee, and for shorter distances from the fairway. The 5 wood can be hit from all lies, using the sweeping stroke for good lies and the downward stroke for tight lies. The 5 wood is a good club from the rough if hit from reasonably good lies.

ADDRESS FOR THE FAIRWAY WOODS

1. Assume a square stance. Keep feet twenty inches apart.
2. Weight should be slightly on the target foot.
3. Place the ball two inches back from the target heel.
4. Keep the hands slightly ahead of the ball.
5. Keep the body square to the target line, and comfortably erect.
6. Flex the knees.
7. Bend from the hips.
8. Take the proper grip.

THE SWING WITH THE FAIRWAY WOODS

The swing with the fairway wood begins with the left arm straight and the right arm soft. Move the triangle of the shoulders, arms and hands straight back from the ball and past the right foot and continue upward to a full backswing.

The wrists will cock naturally no higher than the top of the head. The shoulders will turn fully with the back facing the target. The hips will turn less than the shoulders. The club will point over the right shoulder toward the target.

The downswing begins by turning the hips to the left, causing the weight to transfer to the target leg. This drops the triangle toward the waist and the rear foot as the arms and hands move into the hitting area.

The body stays steady and the triangle swings into the impact area with the left arm guiding and the right hand ready to smash the ball. The swing is down and through the ball. The ball is contacted first and a little turf is taken after contact. A ball sitting up in a good lie will need a sweeping stroke, that does not take turf. The downward stroke is to be used for tight lies. The body position at impact is approximately the same as at address.

As the swing continues through impact and on toward the target, the right arm straightens and the left arm folds into a naturally high follow-through. The swing has been done around the spine. The address posture stays the same throughout the swing. As the triangle moves downward in the downswing, the right shoulder moves down and under as the triangle moves toward impact and the follow-through.

SUGGESTIONS FOR BETTER FAIRWAY WOOD SHOTS

1. Practice fairway wood shots from a driving range or a practice fairway. Practice hitting from good lies and tight lies. Try to land all shots close together.

2. Remember that the objective of the fairway wood shot is to place it in position for an easy iron shot to the green. A loss of backspin in fairway wood shots makes it hard to hold the ball on the green, but try to land the ball on the green anyway.

3. Swing fairway woods in a relaxed way. Trust the club to move the ball and never try for anything extra.

4. Keep the wrists high and straight at address and keep them straight throughout the swing. Keep the body posture steady, with no tilting or dipping during the backswing, downswing and follow-through; to do otherwise spells disaster.

5. Realize that the proper path of the club head in the hitting area moves the club from inside the target line, along the target line and back inside the target line. The club head should never pass outside the target line. If this happens the club head will cross the ball, causing an off-line shot.

6. Remember that the basic fundamentals of the golf swing are the same for every shot in golf. The swings are affected only by the length of the club.

7. Let the club head contact the ball and then the turf, when hitting fairway woods off hard dry areas of the fairway with little grass. Squeeze the ball off the turf. The swing is downward, taking a little turf after contacting the ball.

8. Use fairway wood clubs for the shots on tight driving holes.

9. Choke down an inch on the club shaft to hit soft 4 and 5 wood shots to the green.

10. Hit the driver from the fairway, if the lie is perfect, by choking down one-and-one-half inches on the club shaft. The swing is the same as a 3 wood swing.

Stance for fairway wood shots:

• Assume a square stance. Feet are twenty inches apart.
• Weight should be slightly on the target foot.
• Place the ball two inches back from the target heel.
• Keep the hands slightly ahead of the ball.
• Keep the body erect and square to the target line.
• Flex the knees.
• Bend from the hips.
• Take the proper grip.

One-quarter backswing for fairway wood shots:

• Begin the swing with the left arm straight and the right arm soft.
• The triangle moves the club straight back from the ball to the one-quarter position.

One-half backswing for fairway wood shots:

• The swing continues upward to the one-half position.
• Turn the body around a steady spine.

Full backswing for fairway wood shots:

• Use a three-quarter backswing for fairway wood shots.
• Point the club over the right shoulder toward the target.

One-half downswing for fairway wood shots:

• Begin the downswing by turning the hips to the left. This causes the weight to transfer to the target leg. This drops the triangle toward the waist.

Three-quarter downswing for fairway wood shots:

• The swing continues down. The arms and hands move into the hitting area.

Impact for fairway wood shots:

• The swing is down and through the ball.
• Contact the ball first so a little turf is taken after.
• Keep the body postion at impact approximately the same as at address.

One-half follow-through for fairway wood shots:

• The swing through impact continues on out toward the target.
• Hold the head still in the beginning position.

Three-quarter follow-through for fairway wood shots:

• Straighten the right arm as the left arm is folding.
• Move the right shoulder down and under.

Full follow-through for fairway wood shots:

• Notice that this is a natural, high follow-through.
• The swing should be done around a steady spine.

The Driver—Tee Shots

The driver is the club that will produce the longest shot from the tee. The drive should be placed in position for the best angle for a shot to the green with a fairway wood or an iron. Tight narrow fairways require finesse shots from the tee with the 3 or the 4 wood, depending on the distance needed. The greatest concern in tee shots is to keep the ball in the fairway and, on par 3 holes, to hit the green from the tee.

When standing on the tee, look down the fairway and visualize the best spot to land your drive. Notice any contours that could affect the shot and whether it would be better to place the ball to the left or to the right on the fairway. Keep a mental image of the spot where you want to land the ball as you set up for the shot and retain this image as you execute the swing.

The driver is the easiest club with which to hit. The swing must be coordinated, smooth and in balance, with the proper tempo. The ball cannot move from the tee until the player strokes it with his club.

ADDRESS FOR THE DRIVE

1. Let balance and relaxation start with the set-up for the next shot; they are important in the drive.
2. Assume a stance that is slightly closed, with the feet shoulder width apart. Or, use a square or a slightly open stance.
3. Weight should be slightly on the right foot.
4. Place the ball one inch back from the target heel.
5. Keep the hands slightly behind the ball.
6. Flex the knees.
7. Keep the body square to the target line and comfortably erect.
8. Bend from the hips.
9. Take the proper grip.
10. Tap the heels. The legs should feel alive.

THE SWING WITH THE DRIVER

With the left arm straight and the right arm soft, move the triangle of the shoulders, arms and hands straight back from the ball past the right foot and continue upward to a full backswing, with the wrists cocked naturally above the top of the head. The shoulders will turn fully until the back faces the target but the club will not be allowed to become horizontal at this stage of swing development.

The downswing begins by turning the left hip to the left, causing the weight to transfer to the target leg. This also drops the triangle toward the waist and the rear foot, as the arms and hands move into the hitting area below the waist. The left arm will be guiding and the right arm and hand will be ready to smash the ball.

The swing is down and through the ball. The club head contacts the ball slightly on the upswing, sweeping the ball off the tee. The body stays steady throughout the swing. The body position at impact is approximately the same as it was at address.

The swing continues through impact and toward the target, the right arm straightening and the left arm folding into a natural, high follow-through. The swing is done around the spine. The address posture stays the same throughout the swing. As the triangle moves downward in the downswing, the right shoulder moves down and under as the triangle moves toward impact and the follow-through.

SUGGESTIONS FOR BETTER TEE SHOTS

1. Tee the ball high, with about half the ball showing above the top of the club head when it is soled behind the ball.
2. Check the grip. The back of the left hand should face the target. The palm of the right hand interfaces with the left palm and also faces toward the target. Maintain an even grip pressure throughout all golf swings. Be firm with the last three fingers of the left hand. This will prevent loosening of the grip at the top of the backswing. The firm grip in the right hand should be in the two middle fingers.
3. Practice the wood clubs until you have attained consistency with form and results. Find a good form and repeat it until it is ingrained.
4. Do not stand too close to or too far from the ball. If you do, it will throw your swing off balance.
5. Check the position of the feet; this is important. The left foot is turned one-quarter toward the target and the right foot is turned one-eighth to the right. Many players leave the right foot straight, but this is optional.

6. Keep the right elbow close to the body during the swing. This delays the unhinging of the wrists until the club has reached the hitting area, resulting in greater club head speed and longer distance.

7. Do not ground the club head at address. Keep the club a fraction of an inch off the ground to prevent stubbing on the take-away. This will help set the proper grip pressure and make for a smoother take-away.

8. Prevent swaying by never shifting the weight toward the outside of the feet. The weight should shift to the instep of the right foot during the backswing and onto (not outside) the target foot in the downswing.

9. Counteract centrifugal force in the downswing, by addressing the shot with more weight toward the heels. Maintain the weight there throughout the backswing and the downswing.

10. Face the back of the left hand down the target line as you strike the ball. At address, think of backhanding the club face squarely into the back of the ball. This will result in longer, straighter shots.

11. Increase distance with good timing.

12. Follow this action sequence of the downswing: The left heel lowers and the hips turn to the left, transferring the weight to the left leg; the shoulders turn; the hands and arms start down; the club head moves down past the waist into the hitting area and then through impact and the follow-through.

Stance for tee shots with the driver:

- Assume a stance that is slightly closed. Feet are shoulder width apart.
- Lean weight slightly on the right foot.
- Place the ball one inch back from the target heel.
- Keep the hands slightly behind the ball.
- Square the body to the target line and stay comfortably erect.
- Bend from the hips.
- Take the proper grip.
- Tap the heels; the legs should feel alive.
- Maintain balance and relaxation; they are important in the drive.

One-quarter backswing with the driver:

• The triangle moves the club straight back from the ball to the one-quarter position, with the left arm straight and the right arm soft.

One-half backswing with the driver:

• Turn the body around the spine to move the triangle to the one-half backswing position.

Full backswing with the driver:

• The swing continues upward to a full backswing, with the wrists
  cocked naturally above the top of the head.
• Turn the shoulders full with the back facing the target. The hips turn
  less.

One-half downswing with the driver:

• Begin the downswing by turning the left hip to the left. This causes the weight to begin to transfer to the target leg.
• Notice this also drops the triangle to the waist.

Three-quarter downswing with the driver:

• Move the arms and hands into the hitting area below the waist.

Impact with the driver:

• Guide the left arm as the right arm and hand smash the ball at impact.
• Swing down and through the ball, sweeping the ball off the tee.

One-half follow-through with the driver:

• Contact the ball slightly on the upswing with the club head as it continues to the one-half follow-through position.

Three-quarter follow-through with the driver:

• Move the right shoulder down and under as the triangle moves into the three-quarter follow-through position.

Full follow-through with the driver:

• Notice that the swing has been done around the spine.
• Maintain a steady body throughout the swing.

Suggested Program for Using the Beginner's Instruction Section

1. Learn to putt.
2. Learn to chip with the 5 iron, the 7 iron and the 9 iron.
3. Learn to hit short pitch shots with the 7 iron, the 8 iron and the 9 iron.
4. Learn to hit pitch shots with the pitching wedge, the 9 iron, the 8 iron and the 7 iron.
5. Learn to hit the short irons; the 7 iron, the 8 iron, the 9 iron, the pitching wedge and the sand wedge.
6. Learn to hit the middle irons; the 4 iron, the 5 iron and the 6 iron.
7. Learn to hit the long irons; the 2 iron and the 3 iron.
8. Learn to hit the fairway woods; the 3 wood, the 4 wood and the 5 wood.
9. Learn to hit tee shots with the driver, the 3 wood, the 4 wood and the 5 wood.

Diligent use of the foregoing program in the sequence outlined should produce a sound swing. Practice and playing should produce the skill to break 80 on a par 72 golf course. When you have broken 80, proceed to the advanced golf instruction section (see chapter 4) and work for further progress to any goal you desire to set for your achievement.

Suggested Practice Procedure

At each practice session, try to practice as follows:

1. Putting
2. Chipping
3. Short pitch and pitch-and-run shots
4. Short iron shots
5. Middle iron shots
6. Long iron shots
7. Fairway wood shots
8. Tee shots

The putting, chipping, short pitch shots and pitch shots can be practiced at a practice green.

The short irons, middle irons, long irons, fairway woods and driver can be hit from a driving range. Choose a driving range with an area to hit off the grass. When you have broken 80, establish a handicap and enter some golf tournaments. This will build confidence and help you manage your game on the course.

When you start shooting par, look for USGA amateur tournaments to enter. Amateur champions are often awarded college scholarships. In college, team competition will sharpen your game and upon graduation you may be offered the opportunity to turn professional. A career as a PGA pro could be a worthy goal.

4

THE ULTIMATE GOLF SWING FUNDAMENTALS

This chapter is designed to sharpen your knowledge and skills to achieve the level of proficiency you desire. Therefore, I will begin with a review of the fundamentals.

Instruction for the Advanced Golfer

The Grip

Continue to use the basic grips you have learned. Check to see that your hands work together as one unit. Use a greater grip pressure in the last three fingers of the left hand and the two middle fingers of the right hand. This should prevent loosening of the grip at the top of the backswing.

Check the V's of your grip. The left V should point to the chin and the right V to the right shoulder. Keep the hands high and square throughout the swing with no tilt from side to side or up and down. Keep the body still and steady for a good shot.

The grip must be correct, since no golf shot can be accurate unless the grip is correct to begin with. The next important thing is to have the address correct at the beginning. If both the grip and the address are right, then the backswing, downswing, impact and follow-through are much easier.

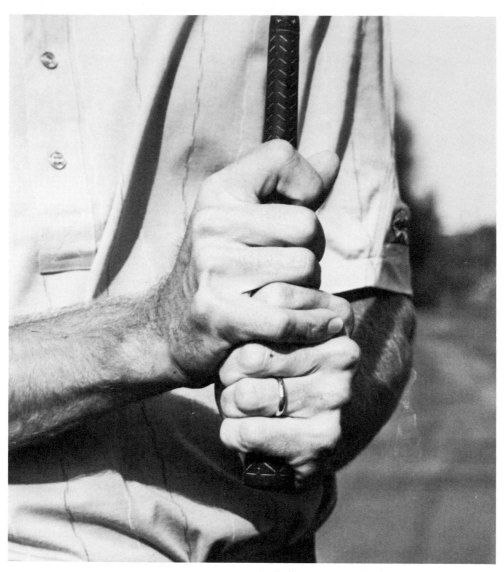

The overlapping grip or Vardon grip. Little finger of the right hand overlaps the forefinger of the left hand.

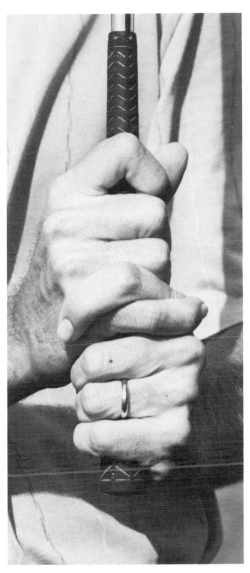 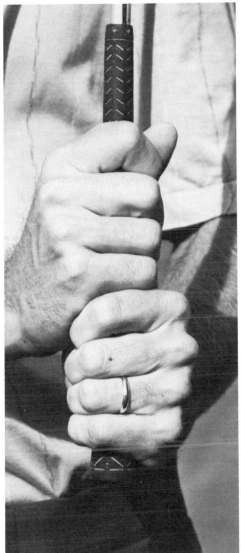

The interlocking grip. The little finger of the right hand interlocks with the forefinger of the left hand.

The baseball grip. All fingers of both hands are on the shaft.

Address for the Drive

1. Keep feet shoulder width apart.
2. Turn target foot left one-quarter turn.
3. Straighten rear foot, or turn one-eighth turn to the right.
4. Flex the knees.
5. Keep the elbows close together.
6. Keep the arms straight but not rigid.
7. Straighten the left arm.
8. Keep the right arm soft.
9. Bend forward from the hips until the weight is on the balls of the feet.

The stance with the driver:

- Assume a stance that is slightly closed. Feet are shoulder width apart.
- Weight should be slightly on the right foot.
- Place the ball one inch back from target heel.
- Keep the hands slightly behind the ball.
- Square the body to the target line and stay comfortably erect.
- Bend from the hips.
- Take the proper grip.
- Tap the heels, so that the legs feel alive.
- Relax and swing in balance.

The Backswing for the Drive

Move the triangle of the shoulders, arms and hands, coordinated with the hips, straight back from the ball and past the right foot. Continue upward to a full backswing. The wrists will cock naturally above the head. The shoulders will turn fully and the back will be toward the target. The hips turn also. The club will point over the right shoulder toward the target. The club may be taken back to horizontal, if that position is comfortable and you are able to manage the club.

Backswing with the driver:

• Move the triangle of the shoulders, arms and hands, coordinated with the hips, straight back from the ball, past the right foot and continue upward to a full backswing.
• The wrists cock naturally above the head. The shoulders will turn fully with the back facing the target. The hips turn also.
• Point the club over the right shoulder toward the target.

The Downswing for the Drive

The downswing begins by turning the left hip to the left, which causes the target heel to lower and the weight to begin to transfer to the target leg. This also drops the triangle toward the waist and the rear foot, as the arms and hands move into the hitting area below the waist. The left arm will be guiding and the right hand will be ready to smash the ball.

The swing is down and through the ball. The club head contacts the ball slightly on the upswing, sweeping the ball off the tee. The body stays steady throughout the swing, so the body position at impact is approximately the same as it was at address.

The downswing with the driver:

- Begin the downswing by turning the left hip to the left, which causes the target heel to lower and the weight to begin to transfer to the target leg. This also drops the triangle toward the waist and the rear foot as the arms and hands move into the hitting area below the waist. The left arm will be guiding and the right hand ready to smash the ball.
- The swing is down and through the ball.

The Follow-Through with the Driver

The swing continues through impact and toward the target, the right arm straightening and the left arm folding into a natural, high follow-through, completely in balance. The swing will have been done around a steady spine (or sternum). The address posture stays the same throughout the swing. As you move through the downswing, the right shoulder moves down and under as the triangle moves through impact and the follow-through.

The follow-through with the driver:

- Continue the swing through impact and out toward the target, the right arm now straightening and the left arm folding into a natural high follow-through, completely in balance. The swing has been done around a steady spine. The address posture stays the same throughout the swing.
- Move the triangle downward in the downswing as the right shoulder moves down and under and the triangle moves through impact and the follow-through.

The Angle of the Back

The angle of the back in the address position is important, and should remain the same throughout the swing, not changing from side to side, or up and down. It must remain at the same angle, turning around the spine, throughout the entire swing. The body position at impact should always be approximately the same as it was at the address.

Target Golf

Concentrate on playing "target" golf. Hit to a spot you have visualized. Just set up, waggle and swing! By this time your swing, timing, tempo and rhythm should be grooved, so I recommend that practice swings be eliminated when you play golf. The time to practice your swing is on the practice green or on the driving range, not on the course. The elimination of practice swings will improve your shots and your confidence. Your play will be quicker, with no wasted motion and the game will be much more enjoyable.

The following is the recommended swing length for:

Chip shots—Take the club back one-eighth of a swing.

Short pitch shots—Take the club back one-quarter of a swing.

Pitch shots—Take the club back one-half of a swing.

Short iron shots—Take the club back three-quarters of a swing.

Middle iron shots—Take the club back three-quarters of a swing.

Long iron shots—Take the club back three-quarters of a swing.

Fairway woods—Take the club back shoulder-high.

Tee shots (driver)—Take the club back head-high.

These swing lengths will provide the best control of the club and the least wear and tear on the back.

The angle of the back at the address:

• Remember the angle of the back in the address position is important and it should remain the same throughout the swing.
• Do not change the angle from side to side or up and down.
• Keep it in the same angle, turning around the spine, throughout the entire swing.

Sand Traps

I have previously recommended that you use pitch shots from sand traps. The following is advanced information on how to hit shots from the sand traps with the sand wedge.

THE EXPLOSION SHOT

1. Assume a slightly open stance.
2. Keep the feet shoulder width apart.
3. Keep the feet dug into the sand for a firm footing.
4. Place the ball one inch back from target heel.
5. Break the wrists quickly on the backswing.
6. Allow the hands to lead the club head in the downswing.
7. Use a firm grip pressure.
8. Keep the club face slightly open.
9. Hit two inches behind the ball.
10. Keep the head still.
11. Follow through, and finish with the left palm downward to keep the club face open during the swing.

The power of the swing will determine the distance, and the object in sand shots is to put the ball near the hole. The texture of the sand also influences distance. Wet or coarse sand will help distance, but dry, powdery sand is hard to escape from and requires a full explosion shot. The "fried egg lie" requires a firm downward swing. Strike the sand two inches behind the ball. Place the ball in line with the rear heel. The club will dig into the sand to lift the ball out of the trap.

The stance for the explosion shot from the sand with a sand wedge:

- Assume a slightly open stance. Feet are shoulder width apart.
- Dig the feet into the sand for a firm footing.
- Place the ball one inch back from the target heel.
- Use a firm grip pressure.
- Open the club face slightly.
- Hit two inches behind the ball.
- Koop the head still.

One-quarter backswing with the sand wedge:

• Break wrists quickly on the backswing.
• Keep the club face open during the swing.

Full (shoulder-high) backswing with sand wedge:

• Determine the distance to put the ball near the hole by the power of
the swing.
• Remember that the texture of the sand also influences distance.

One-half downswing with the sand wedge:

• Lead the club head in the downswing with the hands.
• The body turns around a steady spine.

Impact with the sand wedge:

• The hit is down and through the sand and ball, with the left arm guiding the right arm ready to smash the ball.

One-quarter follow-through with sand wedge:

• Move the triangle through impact into the one-quarter follow-through position.

One-half follow-through with the sand wedge:

• Do not move the head from its starting position. The swing is in perfect balance.

Full follow-through with the sand wedge:

• Finish with the left palm downward to keep the club face open during the swing.

UNEVEN LIES IN THE SAND

Uphill Lie

Position yourself so that the ball is opposite your right toe, when you find the ball in an uphill lie in a sand trap. Your weight should be on your rear foot. Make an outside-in swing, and hit one inch behind the ball.

Downhill Lie

Place the ball so it is opposite the rear heel, with the weight on the target foot, for a downhill lie. Hit two-and-one-half inches behind the ball, and keep your follow-through short.

Chip from the Sand

Hit from a clean lie, to make a chip shot from the sand. Set up as for a regular chip shot, and play the ball near the rear foot. Your weight should be mostly on your target foot. Hit down and through the ball, striking the ball before you strike the sand.

From Fairway Traps

Be sure to choose a club to produce a shot which will clear the lip, from fairway traps. Anchor your feet and make a normal swing. Be sure to contact the ball first, before the sand.

Maintaining the Same Address Routine for All Shots

For each shot you make, first stand behind the ball and note the line and the shot trajectory and locate the target. Select a club for the shot and ground the club face square to your target on the fairway. Imagine a line from the target to the ball. This is the "target line." Then imagine a line from the ball through the feet. This is the "ball line." Put your feet in the proper position, with the target foot slightly to the left and the rear foot at the proper angle. Sight the target again and hold the image in your mind. Waggle and swing!

Make sure that your clubs are clean, the grips are good and your equipment is in good repair. A well-ordered program to maintain your equipment will not only add much to your golfing pleasure but will result in lower scores.

When Hitting All Clubs

When the club head enters the impact area on any swing, the weight will shift to the target foot, allowing a hit "through the ball," with a smash of force toward the target. By halfway through the finish of a swing, the arms should be fully extended and the body posture of the address preserved. When a swing is completed, most of the weight will be on the target foot, and the rear heel will be off the ground. The hands should finish high, with the posture in balance. The body will be facing the target. Allow the angle of the club face to do the work in lifting the ball from the ground.

When hitting all clubs:

• Hold the last three fingers of the left hand firmly on the club to prevent a loose grip during the swing.
• Relax and always keep the head still.

When hitting all clubs:

• Beginners should use a three-quarter swing, when a full backswing is required.
• Players who want to improve their handicaps should use the three-quarter swing.

When hitting all clubs:

- Allow the club face to lift the ball from the ground.
- Shift the weight to the target foot, when the club head enters the impact area, allowing a hit through the ball, with a smash of force toward the target.
- Fully extend the arms, halfway through the finish and preserve the body posture.
- Transfer most of the weight to the target foot, when the swing is completed, and the rear heel will be off the ground.
- Finish high with the hands as the posture stays in balance. The body faces the target at the finish.

Hitting a Deliberate Slice

The slice is used to play around trees or other obstacles. The address for the deliberate slice is as follows:

1. Assume an open stance.
2. Align the open stance to the left of the target line.
3. Aim the club head at the target.
4. Place the ball just ahead of the center of the stance.
5. Swing down the target line.

The swing will be somewhat shortened. The ball will be contacted first at impact, before turf is taken. The slightly open club face will impart a slice to the ball.

Hitting a Deliberate Hook

The hook shot may also be used to play around trees, bushes and other obstacles. The address for the deliberate hook is as follows:

1. Assume a closed stance.
2. Align the stance to the right of the target line.
3. Aim the club head at the target.
4. Place the ball between the target heel and the center of the stance.
5. Swing the club down the target line.

The swing will be somewhat shortened. The ball will be contacted first on impact, before taking turf. The slightly closed club face imparts a hook to the ball.

5

SHOTS FOR PLAYING GOLF

The following is a guide to and review of some of the most frequently used golf shots, along with some strategies for handling special situations you might encounter.

How to Fade
Set up comfortably in a slightly open stance. Aim the club face at the target and swing down the target line.

How to Draw
Set up comfortably in a slightly closed stance. Aim the club face at the target and swing down the target line.

How to Hit the Soft Fade
Address the ball with a slightly open stance, with hips and shoulders turned slightly to the left. Aim the club face at the target. Play the ball near the left heel. Do not let the right hand cross the left until well past impact. Swing down the target line.

How to Hit the Punch Shot
Set up comfortably, with the weight on the target leg. Shorten the grip three inches. Hit down sharply on impact. Contact the ball solidly. This shot will fly low.

How to Hit the Cut Shot

Set up with an open stance. Open the club face and play the ball opposite the target heel. Let the wrists cock fully. This shot is hit from the fairway or from traps around the green.

How to Hook

Assume a closed stance, and play the ball further back than you normally would. Grip to the right, with the left hand on top. V's point to the outside of the right shoulder. Flatten the swing.

How to Slice

Assume an open stance. Play the ball more forward than normal. The grip is to the left and the V's point at the chin. Take the club straight back. Retain left hand dominance.

How to Hit a High Shot

Play the ball forward, opening the club face slightly. Hands are over the club head. Hit the ball at the low point of the swing. Increase wrist action and put more weight on the right foot.

How to Hit the Low Shot

Play the ball further back, closing the club face slightly. Use a shorter, stiff-wristed swing. Have more weight on the target foot and hit down and through.

Rolling Green

Play for slopes nearer the hole to change the direction of the ball more, so slopes have more effect as the ball slows down.

Depressed Green

Approach more boldly, but try for position on the low side of the hole, since a depressed green will tend to make the ball pull up short.

Elevated Green

Approach less boldly, since the ball will have a tendency to run. Pitch for maximum bite, to hold the green.

Wet Green

Stroke the ball more firmly, so putts won't break as far when the green is wet. Move the ball if casual water impedes the course to the cup.

Wet Fairway

Hit the ball first, not the turf behind it. Pick the ball off the grass cleanly and try to keep the ball in the air as long as possible. Approach more boldly, pitching rather than chipping.

Close Lie

Play the ball back slightly. Keep the weight on the target leg. Hit down and through and don't try to scoop. Let the loft of the club face do the lifting.

Hard Wet Sand

Putt or chip the ball if possible. Contact the ball first or use the explosion shot. Use a firmer grip and don't dig as deeply. Follow through.

Explosion Shot

Open the stance and keep the club face open. Plant the feet firmly. Play the ball off the target heel. Keep the hands forward. Make a three-quarter swing, with a full wrist cock. The club face should enter the sand two inches behind the ball. Follow through.

Ball Embedded in Sand

Play the ball back, with the hands ahead of the club head. Square your stance and close the club face. Make your swing more upright and hit more firmly, taking less sand than in the explosion shot.

Heavy Rough

Sacrifice distance to get safely out of the rough. Play the ball centered between the legs. Have a firm grip and a more upright swing. Hit down and through. Contact the ball first and don't scoop.

Long Bunker Shots

Use one more lofted club than you normally would for the same distance. Plant the feet firmly. Play the ball centered between the legs, with the weight on the target heel. Shorten the grip and shorten the swing. Contact the ball first and pick it clean.

Water Hazard

Open the stance and keep the club face open. Use a firmer grip than normal. Enter the water well behind the ball. Be sure to contact the ball before hitting bottom.

Cross Wind

Use one less lofted club than you normally would for the same distance. Tee the ball on the side from which the wind is blowing and play that side of the fairway.

Uphill Lie

Use one less lofted club and aim slightly to the right. Play the ball forward. Bend target knee. Use a low backswing and a straight follow-through.

Downhill Lie

Use one more lofted club and aim slightly to the left. Play the ball further back. Bend the rear knee. Stay down over the shot.

Sidehill Lie (Facing Up)

Use one less lofted club. Shorten the grip, open the stance and keep the weight on the balls of the feet. Aim slightly to the right. Maintain a straight follow-through.

Sidehill Lie (Facing Down)

Use one less lofted club. Stand closer and set down to the shot with the weight on the heels. Keep the hands forward and aim slightly to the left. Stay down over the shot.

Shallow Trap Shots

Putt out, if the trap has no lip. If there is a low lip, chip with a club two numbers higher than usual. Contact the ball first and don't scoop.

Stopping the Ball with the Pitching Wedge

Take a slightly open stance with the feet about ten inches apart. Choke the grip about one inch and play the ball off the target heel. Keep your eyes on the ball, and strike the ball sharply as the club head moves through the ball. The shot should be smooth and crisp. The result is a backspin that will stop the ball on the green.

The iron club face for this shot must be clean, with no dirt or grass to clog the scoring. The scoring imparts a backspin to the ball when the club is swung downward through impact, contacting the ball before taking turf.

Wet Weather Golf

When the weather is wet, play with a slightly wider stance. Keep both feet on the ground when hitting clubs from the short irons through the middle irons. Lift the heel slightly on long iron and fairway wood shots. Pick the ball clean and don't hit behind the ball, because the shot will be ruined and mud will fly.

Try to stay dry as much as you can. Use an umbrella. If possible, wear a rain suit and golf overshoes. Wear a waterproof hat. Take along an extra glove. Keep the glove and the grips of the clubs dry. On the green, hit putts firmly to make certain that they roll to the cup. On the fairway, use sunglasses to keep the mud out of your eyes.

Swing slower and more deliberately. Make solid contact with the ball and expect to lose some yardage. Allow for this loss in planning strategy for playing wet weather golf.

Dry and clean the clubs after a wet round. Dry the bag, the wood covers and all items that become wet.

6

TECHNIQUES

Problems, Causes and Corrections

As you continue to play and learn the game of golf, you may find that you have particular problems with certain shots and techniques. The following guide will assist you in finding possible causes for your difficulties and help you to overcome them quickly.

Problem	Cause	Correction
lack of distance	hitting from the top or uncocking the wrists prematurely	Lead with the hips on the downswing, with the arms and hands following in one piece.

Problem	Cause	Correction
scooping	trying to "lift" the ball by hitting it on the upswing	Keep the hands forward and the weight on the target leg. Hit the ball before taking a divot.

Problem	Cause	Correction
difficulty starting back	lack of preliminary movements	Waggle, sole the club, press forward, then take the club back in one piece.

Problem	Cause	Correction
picking up the club head	right hand dominance	Grip more firmly with the left hand. Start back low, all in one piece, and lead with the hips.

Problem	Cause	Correction
falling forward	poor distribution of weight	Bend the knees and "sit down" to the ball. Keep the weight more on the heels.

Problem	Cause	Correction
moving target foot	lifting the target heel too high on the backswing	Lift the heel only as much as necessary to make the proper pivot.

Problem	Cause	Correction
falling backward	poor transfer of weight	Shift the weight to the rear foot on the backswing, so it can flow left on the downswing.

Problem	Cause	Correction
swaying	moving the body or head from side to side	Coil the body with the head steady.

Problem	Cause	Correction
pushed putts	placing the hands too far in front of the club head	Keep the hands slightly ahead of the club head at impact. The right hand should face the target.

Problem	Cause	Correction
pulled putts	closing the club face after impact	Keep the club face square throughout the stroke.

Problem	Cause	Correction
lack of backspin	trying to "lift" or "scoop" the ball	Hit the ball first, then take the divot. Let the club face do the lifting. Hit down and through.

Problem	Cause	Correction
unable to get out of a trap	taking too much sand or quitting on the shot	Look at a spot one to two inches behind the ball. This is where the club should enter the sand. Follow through.

Problem	Cause	Correction
skying	hitting the ball below the center, chopping the downswing, right hand dominance or having too much weight on the target leg at impact	Start back low, all in one piece. Transfer the weight to the right so it can shift back to the left on the downswing. Keep the left hand firm at the top. Start down with the hips leading and retain the arm and hand action as long as possible. Do not sway.

Problem	**Cause**	**Correction**
pulling the ball straight left of the target	keeping the club face closed to the direction line, square to the outside-in swing, throwing the club from the top or right hand overpowers the left	Shift the weight to the rear leg on the backswing. Make a forty-five degree hip pivot. Keep the head fixed with no sway at the top, and the left hand firm. Point the club head at the target and start down in one piece, hips leading. Shift the weight to the target foot. The arms and hands should follow inside the ball's projected line of flight.

Problem	**Cause**	**Correction**
hooking the ball left of the target	keeping the club face closed to the direction line and the path of the swing, gripping too far around to the right, a flat swing with rolling wrists or right hand overpowers the left on the downswing	Adjust your grip to the left until the first three knuckles of the left hand are visible. The V's should point to the inside of the right shoulder. Start the backswing all in one piece. Let the left arm dominate and keep the left hand firm at the top. Start down, all in one piece, with the hips leading and the wrists cocked.

Problem	Cause	Correction
smothering, so the ball never gets off the ground	the right hand is overpowering the left to the point that the club face is hooded at impact, which eliminates its built-in loft	Adjust the grip to the left, with three knuckles of the left hand visible. The V's should point to the inside of the right shoulder. Keep the left hand firm at the top. Lead the downswing with the hips, while the hands and arms follow in one piece.

Problem	Cause	Correction
topping— hitting above the center of the ball	straightening up, swaying or otherwise changing the arc of the swing; having the weight on the rear leg at impact, which moves the swing backwards	Don't bend too far over or reach for the ball. Stand more erectly. Transfer the weight to the rear leg on the backswing so it can shift to the left in the downswing. Retain the hand and arm action as long as possible.

Problem	Cause	Correction
scuffing— hitting the ground behind the ball	having the weight on the rear leg at impact, or by trying to "scoop," which throws the club head from the top into a chopping downswing	Start the backswing all in one piece, with the head fixed. Let the left arm dominate. Transfer the weight to the rear foot on the backswing so it can shift to the target leg in the downswing. Retain the arm and hand motion as long as possible.

Problem	Cause	Correction
pulled or pushed chips	opening the club face on the backswing and closing on the follow-through	Take a shorter backswing, with firmer wrists and a straight follow-through.

Problem	Cause	Correction
shanking— the ball scoots off the neck of the club	standing too close to the ball, a restricted pivot or an outside-in swing, which throws the club head behind the target line and causes the neck of the club to hit the ball	Stand six inches from the club shaft. Start back all in one piece, with the left arm dominating. Make a forty-five degree hip pivot. Point the club at the target and concentrate on a correct, smooth swing.

Problem	Cause	Correction
pushing the ball to the right of the target	opening the club face to the target line, or a square to inside-out swing	Position yourself so the ball is more forward, so the club face will have time to square itself at impact. Start the backswing all in one piece and don't flatten the swing. Lead with the hips and don't sway.

Problem	Cause	Correction
slicing—the ball curves to the right of the target	opening the club face to the direction line and path of the swing, approaching the ball from the outside-in swing	Adjust the grip to the right so that the first three knuckles of the left hand are visible. The V's should point at the right shoulder. Start back all in one piece, with no sway. At the top, keep the left hand secure. Point the club at the target, lead the downswing with the hips. The arms and hands all in one piece.

Problem	Cause	Correction
fading—the ball starts out straight but picks up a tail-end slice	opening the club face to the direction line and the path of the swing or by gripping too far around to the left	Adjust the grip so that the first three knuckles of the left hand are visible. The V's should point to the right shoulder. At impact, the club face should be square to the target line and slightly closed to the inside-out swing.

Concentration and the Mental Part of Golf

Concentration

Close mental application and/or exclusive attention must be used in managing and executing a golf shot. Golf is a relaxing game, and the walk between holes is to be enjoyed. However, when it is your turn to hit, the pre-shot routine is vital. The short time used in the pre-shot routine is the player's concentration time. This routine must be repeated precisely on every golf shot. A recommended pre-shot routine is as follows:

1. Stand behind the ball and sight down the target line. Locate an intermediate spot for the shot to travel over.
2. Ground the club head with the club face square to the spot on the target line.
3. Imagine a line from the ball to the feet opposite the target line.
4. Move the target foot a short distance toward the target, then move the right foot into position.
5. Sight the target again, waggle and swing.

Concentrate on each part of the pre-shot routine. Don't let yourself be distracted. As you sight down the fairway, visualize the shot and where it will land. Every player would do well to practice visualization on every shot he or she makes, until it is second nature. This process must take place in practice as well as when playing the course. The pre-shot routine is similar to that of tennis, bowling or basketball.

The Mental Part of Golf

Learning to control emotions on a golf course is vital to improving golf scores. Losing one's temper and tightening up will ruin a golf shot. Recovery from fear, nervousness and tension is a part of the game that must be learned if progress toward lower golf scores is to be made.

Every golfer experiences anxiety to some extent in making a shot, but the good golfer learns to control it. Learn to develop a competitive edge. Learn to relax. Increase your powers of visualization and develop a strategic plan for the round you plan to play. Don't respond to pressure. Don't let a bad round create negative feelings. All players experience a bad round occasionally. Think positive and build success in playing golf.

The Warm Up

The purpose of warming up before playing a round of golf is to stretch and loosen the muscles used in the swing. Thirty to forty shots are enough. Start with the short irons, then move on to the middle irons, the long irons, the fairway woods and then the tee shots. Finish up with chip shots, short pitch shots, pitch shots and putts.

Check your swing tendencies, tempo and timing. This should clue you in on the pattern of shots you can expect in the coming round of golf. In the first stages of the warm up, think about your swing. In the last part of the warm up, think of the golf you are going to play.

Begin by making a few shots with your feet together. Try to make solid contact with the ball. Develop good rhythm and wait for the club head to come into the hitting area, through impact and into the follow-through. After this, return to normal shots. If you are short of time and can't hit practice shots, warm up by swinging three clubs together. This will loosen stiff muscles.

If you are right-handed, take several swings from the left side (from the right side for left-handed players). Finish by taking slow backswings and downswings and easy follow-throughs.

When you come to the first tee, remember to swing easily and accelerate through the ball. Relax on all your shots. Tense muscles cannot swing a golf club correctly. Hit a few practice putts, if possible.

Exercises and Drills

1. Swing a twenty-two-ounce training club to strengthen golf muscles and to help groove a swing.
2. Assume the address position without a club. Swing the arms and hands to the top of the backswing. Check that the left knee bends in behind an imaginary ball position, and then swing through impact to a full follow-through. Check to see that the weight transfers to the target leg and the right knee points behind the imaginary ball. Turn around a stationary spine. Keep the head still and swing back and forward until you do this ten times.

3. Assume the address position facing a wall, bend forward and place a small cushion between the forehead and the wall. Swing backward and forward into the backswing and the downswing. Keep pressure on the cushion and turn around a steady spine.

4. Turn a club upside down. Grasp the top and extend the right arm in the address position. Swing the left arm underneath the extended right arm. Pull the left arm through impact and into the follow-through position. Reverse arms and do the same exercise with the right arm.

5. Grasp a rolled-up towel at each end. Assume the address position and swing the arms through the backswing and the downswing. Release the right hand and snap the towel with the left hand in the follow-through.

6. Assume the address position and stretch the arms out straight. Place the right wrist behind the left and apply resisting pressure with the back of the left hand until you can reach the top of the backswing. Reverse the hands and do the same in the downswing.

7. Grasp an iron club at the ends. Place the right hand under and the left hand over in the address position, then make a full swing.

8. Assume the address position and grasp the left arm above the left wrist for the "double hitchhiker." Swing to the top of the backswing with the thumb extended in a hitchhiker position. Swing through downswing to follow through with the left thumb in the hitchhiker position.

9. Lie flat on the floor with the feet together. Then raise one leg and swing it over and up and return it to the floor position. Repeat with the other leg. Be careful to keep the back flat when you swing the legs. Repeat at least ten times for each leg.

10. Stand at attention with the arms at the sides, then raise the arms above the head and swing them in rotation around the shoulders. Repeat at least ten times.

Exercises and drills:

- Stand with the back against a wall with the feet shoulder width apart.
- Place both heels three inches from the wall. Point the right foot straight ahead and point the left foot one-quarter to the left.
- Place the back square against the wall with the head touching the wall.
- Flex the knees so that the body slides one inch down the wall.
- Bend forward from the hips so that the weight moves to the balls of the feet.
- Let the arms hang free and lower the right shoulder so that the right hand can move below the left in the gripping position inside the left knee.
- Tap your heels to make sure you are properly balanced.

Front view of the
address position.

WARM UP EXERCISES

1. Grasp a club at each end and hold it in front of the body. Raise it above the head and lower it behind the back. Extend both arms.
2. Hold a club behind the back in the elbow joints. Turn the body around the spine but keep the feet stationary. Turn back and forth.

Strategy

On the Course

Plan to play well. This is no time to practice. This is the time to shoot the best score possible. This is the way to keep your swing in tune and your score improving.

There are times when a normal shot cannot be made. This is no time to gamble. Make the safe shot which will take the ball back to the fairway. On the fairway, be a hero and hit the next shot to the pin.

Always hit short of a hazard if you have any doubt about clearing it. It is better to be safe, than sorry you have missed a shot. Know the rules; they will save you many strokes. Speed up your game by planning your stance while approaching the ball. Set up square to the target.

When pressure builds, don't tighten up. If you are the underdog, play well and believe that you can beat your opponent. Play only when handicaps are honest.

Leave the driver in the bag when the fairway is tight and the shot calls for accuracy. Always count your clubs when you have completed a round of golf.

Off the Course

Keep records for analysis of your game and your progress. Record such things as the following:

1. The number of fairways hit or missed off the tee.
2. The number of greens you hit in regulation figures. Regulation figures are two shots less than par for the hole. Here are some examples: A par 3 hole should have the ball on the green in one stroke. A par 4 hole should have the ball on the green in two strokes. A par 5 hole should have the ball on the green in three strokes.
3. The number of putts on each hole.
4. The length of the putts together for one round should be added together. Then divide the total by the number of putts. The result will be the average length of the putts you have sunk in that round.
5. The number of times you have gotten down from off the green in two shots.

7

GOLF CONCEPTS AND TERMINOLOGY

Golf Concepts

ARC—The arc of the swing is the invisible path made in the air by swinging the club head. The arc is described by the club head and the length of the club. There will be long arcs and shorter arcs, depending on the length of the club.

The long arc is used with the woods and the long irons. The medium arc is used with the middle irons. The short arc is used with the short irons.

To determine the low point of the arc with an iron, take practice swings until a divot is taken. Practice until turf is taken at the proper spot with the iron you are swinging. This will be the low point of the arc with that iron.

PLANE—The air space within the arc of your swing around the spine, is the plane of the swing. As the swing moves into the backswing, the plane will be upright, flat or in between these two planes. The plane will be determined by the player's height and build.

Set up in a comfortable position, relaxed and balanced. Swing back and accelerate through the ball.

The inside-out plane starts inside the target line, moves along it and then moves inside, in the follow-through. This plane is used with the middle irons.

The outside-in plane starts at the target line, then drifts out and stays outside at impact. This plane is used with short iron shots.

The square plane begins along the target line, moves inside the line and returns square to the ball to a full follow-through. This plane should be used with the long irons and the woods.

The swing has three dimensions; backward, upward and around. These correspond to the backswing, downswing and the follow-through.

Full shots will have length, trajectory, direction and curve. The club head facing must be square at impact. The sweet spot for most

THE THREE BASIC PLANES

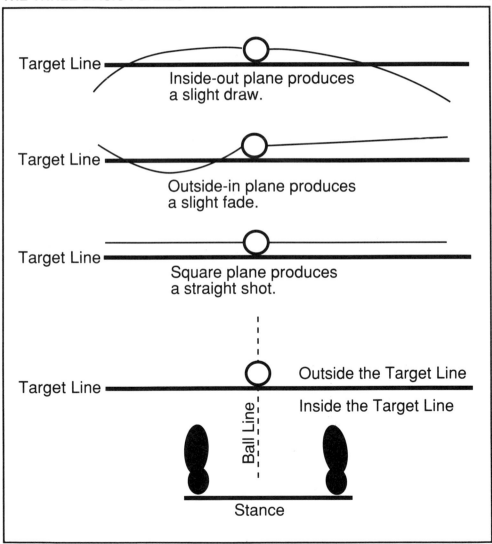

Target Line

Inside-out plane produces a slight draw.

Target Line

Outside-in plane produces a slight fade.

Target Line

Square plane produces a straight shot.

Target Line

Ball Line

Outside the Target Line

Inside the Target Line

Stance

clubs is slightly off center, toward the heel of the club. The club must be swung with the club face square, along the target line. This is the correct path.

The club head moving downward, is the angle of attack that will produce the best shots with the irons and fairway woods. However, the driver should be hit slightly on the upswing.

Terminology

The following are some of the most commonly used terms in general use in golf today:

ADDRESS—Taking the correct stance, flexing the knees and bending from the hips. Aligning the club from behind the ball to the target. Checking the correct grip pressure and preparation for the swing. In a hazard, a player cannot ground the club.

ADVICE—Any counsel or suggestion which could influence a player in determining his play, his choice of club or his method of making a stroke.

ANGLE OF ATTACK—The level angle at which the club moves into the ball.

APPROACH—A shot to the green.

APRON—Grass around the green.

AWAY—Ball furthest from the hole to be played first.

BALL DEEMED TO MOVE—If the ball leaves its position and comes to rest in another lie, it is "deemed to move."

BALL HOLED—The ball is holed when it lies in the cup.

BALL LOST—If the ball cannot be found within five minutes, it is declared lost by the player before five minutes have passed or if after five minutes the player is unable to identify a ball as his ball, the ball is considered to be lost.

BENT—Grass used on greens and tee surfaces.

BEST BALL—A match in which one plays against the better ball of two players or the best ball of three players.

BIRDIE—One stroke under par for a hole.

BOGEY COMPETITION—Stroke play in which golfers play against a fixed score at each hole of a stipulated round or rounds.

BUNKER—A sand trap.

BYE—Unplayed holes after a match is won.

CASUAL WATER—Temporary accumulation of water. This is not a hazard.

CLUB HEAD SPEED—The force applied to the ball at impact.

CLUB HEAD FACING—The square angle the club should be facing at impact.

CLUB HEAD PATH—The path on which the club head is moving at impact.

DEAD—A ball so close to the hole that there can be no doubt that the next stroke will sink it.

DIVOT—Turf removed by a player's club when swung properly.

DORMIE—When a player or side is as many holes up as there are holes left to play.

DOGLEG—A hole that curves right or left to reach the green.

DOWN—In match play, the number of holes a player is behind. In stroke play, the number of strokes a player is behind.

EAGLE—Two strokes under par for a hole.

FAIRWAY—The route of play from tee to green.

FLAGSTICK—A movable pole with a flag placed in the hole to show its location. Also called a pin.

FORE—A yell to warn any player in the way.

FORE CADDIE—Indicates the position of a ball landing on the course.

FOURSOME—Two players play against two, with each side playing one ball.

THREE BALL—A match in which three play against one another, each playing his own ball.

FOUR BALL—A match in which one plays against the better ball of two or the best ball of three players.

GREEN—The putting surface.

GROUND—Touching the sole of the club to the ground at address.

GROUND UNDER REPAIR—Any portion of the course so marked. It includes piled material and holes made by the greenskeeper.

HANDICAP—Strokes allowed to be deducted from par. A player's handicap is computed by the proper handicap system.

HALVED—Players having the same score on a hole.

HOLE—A round receptacle in the green, four-and-one-quarter inches in diameter and four inches deep. Units of play from tee to green. A round consists of eighteen units or holes.

HOLE OUT—Putting the ball into the hole to finish a unit of play.

HAZARD—Water areas and sand traps.

HONOR—The player with the lowest score on the preceding hole tees off first.

HOOK—The ball curves to the left of the target for a right-handed player. The ball curves to the right of the target for a left-handed player.

HOSEL—Extension of the club head into which the shaft fits.

LIE—Position of the ball in the grass or sand. Also the angle of the club shaft to the ground when soled.

LOOSE IMPEDIMENT—A leaf, twig or natural object adhering to the ball.

MARKER—A scorekeeper. Also markers showing limits of the tee-off area on a hole to be played.

MATCH—A contest between two or more players or sides.

MARKER (BALL)—Small coin or a plastic marker used to mark the ball location on the green when the ball is moved.

MATCH PLAY—Each hole produces a winner. The player who wins the most holes wins the match.

MEDAL PLAY—Competition in which results are determined by the number of strokes played.

NASSAU—Players competing in match play or stroke play. The winner is awarded one point for the first 9, one point for the back 9 and one point for 18 holes.

NET SCORE—The total score less the player's handicap.

ODD—A term for the player who has already played one stroke more than his opponent.

OBSTRUCTION—An object erected or placed on the course.

OUT OF BOUNDS—Ground on which play is prohibited.

PAR—Playing the hole in the number of strokes listed on the card for the hole.

PENALTY—A stroke added to the score of a player or side under certain rules.

PROVISIONAL BALL—A second ball hit if the first ball appears to be out of bounds or if the ball lands in a water hazard.

PULL—A straight shot which flies left of the target.

PUSH—A straight shot that flies right of the target.

PUTT—Playing a stroke on the green.

PUTTING GREEN—Ground prepared for putting. All ground around the hole.

ROUGH—Long grass close to the tee, fairway, hazards or greens.

RUB OF THE GREEN—A condition arising when a ball in motion is stopped or deflected by an agency outside the match.

SAND SAVE—Par 3 holes: a shot from the sand that can be canned in one stroke. Par 4 holes: two putts. Par 5 holes: two putts.

SLICE—A shot which curves to the right for a right-handed player or to the left for a left-handed player.

SOLE—Act of placing the club head on the ground at address.

SQUARE—A match that is even.

STANCE—The position of the feet when addressing the ball.

STROKE—The forward motion of the club to impact the ball.

STROKE PLAY—Competition based on the total number of strokes played. Same as medal play.

TARGET—The spot where the ball is expected to land.

TEE—The peg on which the ball is placed on the tee before striking the ball.

TEEING GROUND—The area from which the play on each hole starts.

THREESOME—A match in which one plays against two and each side plays one ball.

THREE BALL MATCH—Three play against one another, each playing his own ball.

TOP—A ball hit above its center.

TWOSOME—One player playing against another.

UP—The number of strokes by which a player leads his opponent in stroke play or the number of holes by which he leads his opponent in match play.

WINTER RULES—Local club rule (not part of USGA rules) allowing the player to move the ball with the club head to a better lie, but not nearer the hole.

WAGGLE—Preliminary action, swinging the club backward and forward.

WHIFF—Missing the ball entirely.